Mrs. Bacon

Duckey and the Ocean Protectors

By John Sexton and Katie Gutierrez

Illustrations by Maciej Zajac

Duckey and the Ocean Protectors

By John Sexton & Katie Gutierrez
Illustrations by Maciej Zajac

ISBN: 978-0-981454573

Library of Congress Control Number: 2008935797

Published By:

1670 Valencia Way
Mundelein, IL 60060
Phone: 224.475.0392
www.writersoftheroundtable.com

Cover Design and Interior Layout by:
Nathan Brown
Writers of the Round Table Inc

This book is dedicated to all the inhabitants of our oceans and to every person, young and old, who pitches in to keep our largest natural resource clean, healthy, and safe for all of us.

pRologue

the massive great white shark woke up to the blinding light. He moaned and clenched his eyes shut, trying to turn his back to the persistent glare, but it didn't matter—it was everywhere. He never really slept anymore. Not like he used to in the ocean, anyway. Day after day the light blared in his small tank, where clear walls surrounded him. Swimming back and forth along the seamless glass, never giving up on finding some clue for escape, he could barely make out the odd upright shapes of humans, almost constantly coming and going. Sometimes he bared his teeth in a painful grimace, trying to scare them, but they seemed more amused than frightened. It was usually then that he caught a slight glimpse of his own reflection in the glass. What were those strange things on his head? He lowered his nose and scraped and butted against the tank, but it was no use and only made his headache worse. Whatever those things were, they weren't coming off.

The shark didn't know how long he had been there. His memories seemed hazy, at best. He felt lost in an almost constant blur of the light, the searing pain behind his eyelids, the feeling that his head was heavier than it used to be, and the all-consuming worry about his family. His family! How he tried to remember them, but the only images he could capture were of darting in and out of the cavernous, old shipwreck they called home.

One scene played over and over again in his mind. It was the day his life changed forever: he called his brother Sam and best friend Stan back down into the deep waters where it was safer. As he swam, his mom's words ran through his mind—"Avoid humans…stay deep and only play around the ship." But as he turned the corner in a game of hide-and-seek, he saw men in diving suits, and turned in panic to see the look of horror in Sam's and Stan's eyes. The shark called for his parents and thrashed to fight the net that was falling all around him. When something sharp hit him in the belly, everything went dark. Now, he never stopped wondering if he would see home again…or ever even be able to remember his own name.

One night, a woman's voice startled the shark awake. A light came on, but it wasn't *the* light. It didn't surround him; it was dimly orange like the sun breaking through the ocean at the end of the day.

"Look at you," the woman's voice said softly. She sounded sad, speaking in muffled tones through the glass. "Those…horns. What have we done to you? This isn't right."

The shark struggled to keep his eyes open. Even the soft light hurt them now.

"No more experiments for you. I'm going to take you back," the woman said, a little more certainly. "So what if I get fired? I can't let this happen anymore."

The light went off again, and the shark burrowed back into the darkness, more comfortable now. He didn't understand—didn't know what the woman meant—but her voice sounded kind—like his mother's. He fought back the tears in his eyes and thought of home again.

The next night, the woman came back. All in darkness, the shark steeled himself as the tank started shaking. His body swayed in the water and tossed against the sides as the tank moved. The woman kept saying, "It's okay, it's okay," in a soothing voice, and even though she was a human, the shark found himself starting to feel like he could trust her.

After what seemed like days, the shark heard something familiar: the surf! He listened intently to the waves crashing against each other on the beach and the shrill cries of seagulls. A motor thrummed to life, and the tank shook again, then steadied. Were they on a boat? For a moment, he could almost pretend he was in the ocean, his body moving back and forth with the current. Despite the suspense, the humming motor and steady movement lulled him into a light sleep.

He woke up when the motor cut out. *What now?* he thought, squinting.

Then, the heavy metal lid above his head lifted—little by little. Suddenly, a flash of lightning frightened him and a clap of thunder vibrated through the water ever so slightly. He turned his body, going as deeply as he could, thinking he was in for more of the torturous light. "It's okay," he heard the woman say. He saw her smiling face and edged closer to the surface. "Almost there." She paused and looked right into his eyes. "My friend. You had a number for a name back at the lab, but this storm appeared when I lifted the lid here to set you free, so I will always remember you as Raiden, God of Thunder…Raiden." She said the word a couple more times. Then, something whirred, and the tank moved again and began to lower…into the ocean! She was taking him back home!

The shark's chest ached with joy, and he circled around in excited, tight little circles in the tank. The woman laughed. "I know, you're ready, huh?" she asked. She said something else, but he couldn't hear because right then, water crashed through the open lid, and he hurled himself up and out. As suddenly as he'd been caught, he was free! Free in the vast, swirling waters without walls! Free to find his family again!

"*Yes!*" the big shark yelled, swimming in a fast, wide circle around the woman's boat. He felt like a child again. "*Yes!*"

When he calmed down, he finally looked up toward the boat, trying to get a good look at the woman. Through the wavy lens of the water, he saw his beautiful rescuer, leaning over the side of the boat, looking down at him with a bright, wide smile. Her long, shiny black hair was pulled back, letting the moonlight glint off her cheeks, and her big almond eyes sparkled. Even though he knew he'd never see the woman again, he'd never forget her face. She waved, and he wished he had a hand to wave back.

With a final glance backward, he plunged deeper into the ocean, swimming as fast and hard as he could back to the ship (or at least where he thought the ship was—he was never much good at directions). Finally, after what seemed like eons later, he reached the bright orange buoy that marked—ironically—the territory off-limits to divers. Breathlessly, he surged past, shooting into the ship that felt heavy with silence.

"Mom! Dad! Sam! Stan!" he yelled. Half blind, he sped through the ship's corridors and ballrooms, even squeezing through some of the smaller cabin doors. But no one called back, and dread seeped through his body. Where was everyone?

"Mom!" he screamed again from the middle of the ship. "Mom, please! I'm back!"

All his time away, though he had come close, he had never really shed any tears. Great white sharks didn't cry, Dad always said. But now he felt even more alone and far more hopeless than he had in the humans' tank, and he had to snarl to choke back this devastated feeling. The ocean was so vast…how would he possibly find everyone that he loved?

A noise sounded from one of the ship's corridors, and his head jerked up, every nerve on alert. He half expected to see the divers, back to reclaim him, but instead, a shark cautiously glided into the ballroom.

"Sam!"

"Jimmy!"

The name sounded strange to the big shark, so long without any memory of it. He paused and looked questioningly at Sam.

"What's wrong? It's me!" Sam exclaimed.

"I...I know..." the big shark said. "It's just..."

"Aw, come on!" Sam said, racing toward his long lost brother. They collided, bouncing backward from one another, and then pushing against each other again, their teeth bared in ecstatic grins.

When they'd finally calmed, Sam was staring at the strange horns protruding from his big brother's head. "Ah, these..." he said, embarrassed. "I'll tell you later. Mom and Dad—where are they? I have so much to tell..."

Sam's eyes were hard, bottomless.

"Sam...where are Mom and Dad?"

"They went after you," Sam said flatly. "They tried to follow the boat." Sam could not say anything more and then just shook his head and cast his eyes towards the bottom of the ocean.

His brother blinked at Sam's words. Then the meaning hit, slamming into him with more force and more pain than the humans could ever inflict with their tools. *It's my fault. It's all my fault*, he thought over and over again. He turned away from his brother for a moment.

"Jimmy...that was my name, wasn't it?"

When he turned back, he had a glare of determination in his eyes, and Sam nodded.

"Well, everything is different now. Don't call me that. Call me Raiden. My name is Raiden."

Chapter One

Denise Dolphin had just slipped out the gates of her tank at Sea World, the way her parents had taught her when she was much younger. At seven feet long, two hundred and fifty pounds, and never without the latest fashion, Denise was beautiful and she knew it. "The only blue dolphin off the coast of Miami," her trainers liked to boast. They made sure that her dark back gleamed when she flew out of the water, pure white underbelly flashing on return. Her turquoise eyes sparkled like the ocean itself. But after a day performing for her thrilled fans at the theme park, the only home she had ever known, Denise suddenly felt the need to be by herself for a little while. Every superstar needed her quiet time.

She laughed, clicking happily. The water was perfect today—warm where the sun hit it and cooler in the darker, shadowy parts. She loved the feel of the endless ocean all around her. What a difference from her tank! She laughed again, throwing herself out of the water in a high flip. She wondered if anyone had seen her joyously performing one of her best tricks.

When she dove back in the water, she thought she heard something strange…a Gloria Estefan song? Worried, she glanced back toward the gates. Had one of the trainers noticed she was gone? Or had she simply imagined the music? After all, the song seemed to be coming from under the water, not from the huge speakers above. She spun around in a quick circle, trying to identify the source of the sound.

Then it stopped, and all was quiet. Denise stayed very still until she heard a melodic voice: "Denise, I have something important to tell you." It would have scared the daylights out of her (she was already thinking she might be crazy) if the voice weren't so pretty! But she still couldn't tell where it was coming from.

Someone giggled.

Denise whirled around again and finally saw her—a snail-like creature with a perfect spiral shell, heavy mysterious eyes, and a playful smile. "How do you know my name?" Denise asked the creature.

"Oh, that doesn't matter right now. But if you care to know mine, it's Nicky. Nicky Nautilus."

"Nicky?"

"Yes. Now, come closer. I need to show you something…something you may not believe."

Bewildered but curious, Denise Dolphin swam closer to Nicky Nau-

tilus, who was reaching far, far back in her cream and brown shell. With a quiet grunt, she finally pulled out a large, ornate hand mirror. The gold should have been dull from being in the ocean (and Nicky's shell!), but instead, it shone with a radiance that Denise had never seen before. She gazed at Nicky Nautilus in awe.

"Don't look at me," Nicky scolded teasingly. "Look into the mirror."

Denise Dolphin did--and after a few moments she flew from the water in her highest flip yet. This time, though, it was from shock.

Polly Puffer Fish needed to escape!

Everything was a blur as she swam faster than she ever had before. She'd seen it, seen the shark, less than a mile back! She didn't think it had seen her, but you never could tell. Those sharks were sneaky, mean creatures. Just when you thought you were safe, hiding behind a clump of coral or finally out of its sneaky, sneaky radar, *gulp!* You were gone! She'd never known anyone personally who'd been caught by a shark, but you had to be on your guard at all times! So she wasn't taking any chances. She would swim until she was in a whole different ocean if she had to, or until she passed out from exhaustion—as long as she escaped.

After awhile, Polly took a risky, hopeful glance behind her. All empty ocean. Just schools of little fish, even littler than her, but much brighter. She wished she could be brighter. Electric blue would be nice, she thought. Much better than her boring sandy color. Then she remembered what she was looking for and

got scared all over again. She should keep moving. But it was so nice where she was at, all calm and cool…

"Polly!"

"*Aiiigh!*" Polly Puffer Fish shrieked in terror, puffing out to twice her normal size, spikes poking out defensively. She burst into another blind beeline away from…the shark? But how would the shark know her name? And the voice was a girl's voice. Not that there weren't girl sharks, but Polly had never been chased by one of those before.

Still, she couldn't take any chances.

"Polly! Slow down, will ya?"

Hmm…the voice was sounding a little irritated. Irritated, but not, well, *hungry.* Polly turned around cautiously.

"You're a hard girl to catch up with!" said the owner of the voice, a pretty nautilus whose clean curvy shell seemed to be emitting a kind of music. Her big brown eyes looked both wise and amused.

"Really?" Polly asked, pleased. "Because me practice—"

"Okay," the nautilus laughed. "No time for chats. I'm Nicky Nautilus. And I need to show you something pretty incredible."

Polly Puffer Fish watched questioningly as Nicky Nautilus disappeared into her shell. "That trick neat," Polly said. And it was. But why would this stranger, Nicky Nautilus, chase her for half an ocean just to show her that?

Nicky's head popped out again, and she smiled. "That's not what I have to show you, Polly," she said kindly. "Here. Look at this."

Polly got really close to Nicky to see what she was holding: a lovely mirror (that looked pretty heavy). The gold flashed brightly, as if the sun had struck it. But they were still in the cool shady depths. "What…?" Polly Puffer Fish started to ask—and then couldn't say anything at all. She was too amazed by what the large, mysterious mirror showed her.

"I'm going to beat you this time, Kilo!"

Kilo Killer Whale laughed, a deep warm rumbling from the bottom of his massive belly. His brother Kiley said that every time they played this game.

"Think again, Kiley!" he shouted back.

"Or maybe I'll win today!" came the sweet voice of their little sister, Kelly. At this, all three of them laughed. Kelly had even less chance of winning than Kiley; everybody knew that. But it was still fun to play.

The three whales were just under the surface of the Bering Sea, their home and favorite place in the world, even though they had traveled to plenty of other places. They were each positioned at the end of three huge, enormously heavy icebergs. The game? To see who could push his or her iceberg the farthest.

Seventeen feet long and weighing in at over a ton, Kilo had won the game for as long as he could remember. He was always the one who was most surprised by his effortless strength; after all, he was only twelve years old and could already send five thousand-pound bergs flying across the ocean. Today, though, he decided to let one of the others win. He knew how happy it would make them—even if they never let him hear the end of it.

"Ready!" Kilo shouted. "Set! Go!"

He pushed his considerable weight against his iceberg, though not as hard as usual, glancing sideways at Kiley and Kelly. They each had a look of utmost concentration on their faces, and Kelly's tongue was poking out of the corner of her mouth. Kilo smiled to himself. He hoped she'd win.

But even though he was holding back, his iceberg made a loud cracking noise and careened forward in a crazy, powerful pattern. Unfazed, he called out, "Check!" In quick streaks of black and white, all three whales hurried toward their icebergs to measure whose had gone farthest.

Kilo won.

"Not again!" grumbled Kiley good-naturedly. He threw himself into Kilo, and the two playfully tumbled around underwater to the sound of Kelly's infectious laughter.

"Kilo!"

"Yeah, Kelly?" he called out, pushing Kiley away with a grin.

"I didn't say anything," Kelly said, swimming up to her brothers. Her brown eyes were bright and joyful.

"Yes, you did," agreed Kiley.

"No, I didn't!"

"Well, *somebody* called me!" Kilo exclaimed, catching his breath and looking around.

"Yeah," said a tiny, melodic voice. "I did!"

All three whales looked around, confused, before Kilo's gaze finally landed on a girl snail, floating right in front of his face. She was so small,

Kilo at first thought she was an air bubble.

"Come with me, Kilo," she said, and Kilo Killer Whale thought he saw her tiny teeth chattering. He shrugged at Kiley and Kelly, who were looking on curiously. "There's something you need to see," the snail added.

"Okay…" Kilo said uncertainly. "Um…can I give you a ride?" he asked.

A look of pride flashed over her face before she said dryly, "Sure. Why not. It'll be faster this way." She perched on Kilo's side, and he slowly (for him) swam away from his siblings.

"Stop here," she soon said, sliding off of Kilo. She disappeared into her shell without another word, and Kilo was worried for a second that she was so cold she wouldn't come back out. When she did, however, she was holding a mirror at least five times her size. Kilo squinted. *How did she fit that thing in her shell?*

"Look," she said simply. "I'm Nicky. Nicky Nautilus. And I am *not* a snail," she added with a dazzling smile.

How did she know what he was thinking? He was about to apologize and introduce himself when he remembered (duh) that she already knew who he was—and then the mirror flashed a bright gold…and started speaking to him in a voice that he'd only heard in legends:

"Hello, Kilo Killer Whale. For your great physical strength and your pure heart, I have chosen you for a mission that will change the world."

Kilo gasped, looking at Nicky Nautilus. She, too, was focused on the mirror that she held before them both.

"It won't be easy," the voice continued from the mirror. "There are those who will try to stop this revolution for their own gain or because of their own ignorance. But I have faith in you, Kilo…you will learn more about this mission soon. Very soon."

With that, the mirror became just a mirror again, and Nicky slid it back into her shell without a word. Again, Kilo wondered how such a small creature could store such a large object within her shell. What else did she have in there?

"So," Nicky said finally, quietly. "Will you join our team?"

Kilo's hundred-pound heart was pounding excitedly. *A mission that will change the world...* what could it be? It seemed like a wild, fantastic dream that *he* would be called to join this group, this team—but no matter what the risk, he couldn't turn away now. He looked to where he knew Kiley and Kelly were waiting curiously. And then he thought dizzily, this mission was *for* them! For everyone he loved.

"Yes!" he said solemnly, then broke the big silence with another of his thunderous laughs, so deep it seemed to shake the whole ocean. "Yes, Nicky! You bet I will!"

Nicky Nautilus smiled at him widely. "Good," she said. Her teeth were definitely chattering this time. "Now I can move on to warmer waters! I'll be seeing you again soon, Kilo Killer Whale." And with that, she was off, floating away from him with surprising speed.

Chapter Two

School had just let out, and it was a beautiful sunny afternoon. The pond shone brightly, throwing startling prisms of light into the sky as my classmates played races from one end to the other. My twin sister Deb was in the lead, as always, and my brothers were hollering their encouragement from the sidelines. As for me, I was in the boathouse apart from everyone, doing what I love most: writing.

Hunched over my typewriter, a gift from Mom and Dad a few years ago, I didn't even hear someone swim up behind me. I must have jumped three feet in the air when a hand touched my shoulder—if only I could do that in a basketball game!

"Dad!" I exclaimed.

He smiled at me, his eyes all warm and serious. *Parents. What can you do?* I grinned back. He was holding the big bowl that was usually full of carrot sticks, still my favorite snack, on our kitchen table. Mom must have asked him to bring it over; she believed that I should have nourishment while I worked. (Between you and me, she still thinks I'm five, but I indulge her cause I'm a good kid!) When I reached for the bowl, Dad

pulled back.

"Today is a very special day," he said mysteriously.

"Every day is a special day," I sarcastically reminded him. That was something Mom had always told us before bed: *Goodnight, little ones. Sleep well; tomorrow is another special day.* Seriously, fiction wouldn't be nearly this boring.

"Yes," my father continued. "But today is different."

He placed the bowl carefully on my desk, and I leaned over, peering inside. No telltale orange glow along the rim, and definitely no carrot sticks. Instead, there was a single clam, the same size and grey-brown color of most of the rocks around the pond. I looked back up at Dad, who was still smiling like he had a secret. Honestly, I found the situation a little ridiculous.

"Son, finish that article you're writing as soon as you can…because you've just gotten another assignment that's much, much bigger," Dad said.

My heart started to pound the way it always did when I got a new assignment. It's the kind of excitement you get when you're about to open a birthday present and you're thinking that it could be *anything* underneath that wrapping paper and tissue. Maybe even the thing you want the most, like a new comic book or a sweet pair of inline skates. Now *this* I could dig.

"What's the assignment?" I asked in a hushed tone.

Dad nodded to the bowl. "Listen carefully to what you're about to hear. It's imperative that you don't miss a single word of this story."

I looked skeptically at the clam, thinking Dad was making one of his lame "Dad" jokes. Everyone knew clams didn't talk. At least not to us ducks. What kind of story would a clam be able to share, anyway? How to make the most of cramped spaces?

"Just listen," Dad said, as if he could read my mind. He gave a last, long look at the clam before adjusting his top hat (Dad's silly trademark) and walking out the door. I watched until he made it to the pond and hopped easily into the water, cutting across in one clean, smooth motion, as if he had a motor propelling him forward. I wished I could swim like that.

My thoughts were broken by a rattling sound in the bowl. I turned back and watched in disbelief as the clam shook itself against the bowl's sides, like it was trying to get my attention. Then its eyes popped open and it said in a deep, friendly voice: "Hello, Duckey! I'm Christopher."

I shook my head and looked around. My brother Danny must've planned a joke. Were he and my sister hidden somewhere, waiting for my reaction? But there was no one nearby. Everyone had cleared out of the pond; I couldn't even hear any voices. It was just me and, well— the Clam.

"Hello," I said uncertainly. "I didn't know oysters could talk."

"I'm not an oyster! I'm a clam!"

"Right, that's what I meant." I looked at him more carefully. I had said *oyster* accidentally, but he actually did look like an oyster. "Well, there's not much of a difference, is there?"

He rolled his eyes like he'd heard this a million times. "Just like there's no difference between a duck and a goose," he grumbled. "But, *anyway,* there's no time for long greetings or lessons in telling drastically different animals apart. We have work to do!"

Maybe now would be a good time to tell you who I am. My name is Duckey Jr., though I prefer to be called The Duckster. My dad is Duckey, Sr. He's a newspaperman—the owner of *Duckey Daily,* our community paper. He would never say it, but he's pretty important around here. Without him and our paper, no one would ever know what was going on around the pond—which areas are being treated for pollution, who's new to the neighborhood, who's won the latest basketball game, things like that. Everyone would have to figure stuff out on their own, and it'd sure be a lot harder to share that information without a newspaper.

Dad's always told us that all knowledge is stored in the written word. That's a big responsibility for us writers. See, at the time I met Christopher, I wrote a column for *Duckey Daily* myself. I covered all types of pond activities, but mostly sports. While some of the other ducks around got the brawn, I got the brains, so I was always trying to use 'em—and I took my job seriously. After all, it wasn't easy to be the best at something, like running or swimming or basketball, and those who were (usually Deb) deserved recognition.

That day, though, my job looked like it could take a very different turn, expanding my world more quickly than I could write about it—and sending me what Christopher described as the greatest adventure of my life.

"Someone very special and *very* powerful chose you for this assignment," Christopher said softly. "*You,* specifically, Duckey. He's read your work, especially the article you wrote about beach erosion."

I couldn't help a proud grin. A few months back, I had written an article for my school paper about how to use Christmas trees to protect beach ecosystems. I had never visited a beach before in my life, which Dad said made the article that much more amazing. That was when he offered me my own column in *Duckey Daily*. I felt a chill of pride under my feathers.

"So what is it?" I asked, with a touch of skepticism. "What's the assignment?"

"I'm going to tell you a story," Christopher said with a smile. "A story of bravery and adventure...one that could change the future of everyone on this earth." He looked at me closely. "It's your job to put the story in writing and get it into people's hands—and hearts."

"Come on," I scoffed. "You're kidding, right?" Like I was about to believe a clam?

"Actually, I'm not, Duckey. Are you in, or are you out?"

I thought about it long and hard. Something didn't seem to be adding up, but I didn't feel I could pass up the chance of a lifetime if this was actually for real. "I'm in. For now," I added as I put another piece of paper into my typewriter. "And call me The Duckster!"

The ocean's surface was bubbling with excitement—literally. Little Polly Puffer Fish couldn't help exhaling large bubbles that kept bumping into the other three creatures grouped curiously together. Blowing bubbles was something she'd always done, whether in excitement, nervousness, or fear—and today, she felt something like a combination of the three. It was, after all, the most important day of her life...so far.

Next to Polly floated the biggest creature she'd ever seen; it would take her two days just to swim around that killer whale. But he seemed nice, she thought. He had a soft, kind smile and kept mostly to himself, just watching everyone else with his deep brown eyes that were five times the size of Polly's entire body. A little ahead of them was a bright, gleaming, blue dolphin who seemed pretty excited. She kept whirling around in her silky colorful blouse. She was spinning faster and faster, creating a miniature whirlpool.

"Hey!" said Nicky Nautilus a bit crossly. She wrapped her hands around the mouth of her shell, as if to hold herself inside. "Denise! You're going to drag me into that thing!"

Denise Dolphin laughed merrily. "Oh, Nicky. Loosen up!" She winked and started whirling in the other direction, shooting a spray of seawater into the air.

"You may want to watch it with that spout," came another voice, amused and mellow. "You could throw a guy into the clouds—which would be kinda cool, actually."

The voice perfectly matched its owner. As Polly watched in amazement, a sea otter in baggy surf shorts rode up to the group, confidently perched atop a red surfboard. "Where's the party?" he said, flipping his sunglasses to the top of his head. "I'm Murdock—*not* the 'short hairy guy who surfs,' as the people in Cali know me. Anyone know what to expect here?"

Someone laughed from above the water's surface. Through the water, Polly saw a big seagull gliding gracefully, then swooping down almost low enough to touch her. She blew a bubble in fright.

"I don't know what to expect, but I sure flew a long way to find out!" the seagull said in a thick, rolling Scottish brogue.

"Did you come from farther away than California? 'Cause that was a hell-o-wave to catch," Murdock Sea Otter said, flopping down casually on the surfboard. He let his short arms dangle into the water.

"A wave?" Scotty Sea Gull rolled his beady eyes. "All *you* had to do was ride; I had the much more complex task of finding the right wind, catching food along the way—"

"Food!" Polly Puffer Fish gasped, wide-eyed.

Everyone turned to look at her, and she could feel her body expanding in embarrassment, making a bubble of itself, so to speak. The whale nudged her with a fin and smiled, showing a huge mouthful of rounded teeth. "Don't worry," he said. "Puffer fish wouldn't make good meals for gulls. Just look at you! He'd be scared to go near you with those spikes!"

She smiled gratefully. "Me Polly," she said, relieved.

"I'm Kilo Killer Whale," he replied, and Polly edged closer to Kilo, her new friend.

"And I'm Scotty," the seagull declared. "From Scotland. And I *don't* eat puffer fish."

At that moment, the ocean began churning and rumbling, and even Denise Dolphin became absolutely still as the water around her shook. Her turquoise eyes sparkled in anticipation. With a noise like thunder, a figure rose to the surface in the middle of the creatures' circle, and everyone gasped in wonder. It was *him*. Water dripping like diamonds from his golden-red beard, chest as broad as two human men, there he was... the legendary Ruler of the Seas.

"Hello, my friends," King Neptune bellowed. His voice was deep and smooth like sandworn stones at the bottom of the ocean. "Please, come closer."

Polly Puffer Fish, Kilo Killer Whale, Denise Dolphin, Nicky Nautilus, Murdock Sea Otter, and Scotty Sea Gull surrounded King Neptune in awe. They thought of all the stories they had heard of the great ruler, dating back thousands and thousands of years, to when humans used to recognize his mighty power. Seamen trusted him to keep them safe, even on roiling, stormy waters. They built statues and wrote books honoring his greatness. And King Neptune kept his word. He guarded the seamen and the wild, frothy oceans on which they traveled. But little by little through the years, humans seemed to forget about King Neptune, forget about how he had risen from the seas to protect them from cyclones, earthquakes, and tsunamis. Now, humans considered him only a myth, a

story. But the sea creatures had always known different. They knew that King Neptune still ruled supreme—and now there he was, right in front of them.

"Nicky has revealed a little of your mission," Neptune said, once they had all formed a tight semi-circle around him. "Now it is time to tell you everything.

"As you know, I draw my power from the Diamond of the Seas,

which I have kept safe in my palace for a millennia. Through the Diamond, I can communicate with any creature I choose, see through to all of the oceans' hidden nooks, and even change form as needed." Neptune paused, wrapping his massive hands around his trident. He met each one of their eyes. "The Diamond has been stolen."

There were audible gasps around the circle.

Neptune continued, "And I have called all of you together to find it and bring it back."

"How—" Scotty Sea Gull squawked.

"What—" Denise Dolphin gasped.

"But—" Murdock Sea Otter yelped.

"Quiet!" Neptune roared, and the group lapsed back into silence with wide eyes. "I didn't say that your task would be easy. But it's essential. Without the Diamond, I will continue to weaken until I have no powers left at all—and if that happens, I will be unable to protect these oceans we call home." Neptune paused, his face softening. "Listen closely. I chose you all to retrieve the Diamond because each of you has a special, unique talent that will be required to carry out this mission…with the very last of my powers, I have enhanced that talent within each of you to aid you in this mission."

Denise got out, "What 'talents?'" when Polly said quietly, "Me not strong." Her little round eyes were downcast.

Kilo opened his mouth, but Neptune held out a hand. With a start, they all saw that the massive hand, brown as damp sand, was shaking. Kilo looked quickly to Neptune, and Neptune nodded grimly, understanding Kilo's alarm.

"Yes, you are," Neptune said to Polly Puffer Fish, rubbing one thick ginger eyebrow as though his head was aching.

Polly smiled, but she didn't look at all convinced.

"I need to return to my palace to rest," Neptune said. "Remember: the Diamond is losing strength every moment—so you'll need all of your talents together to find it."

What about you? Denise wanted to cry. *What about your strength?* Her throat felt tight with tears. She hated to think of Neptune weakening. If there was one thing she had always counted on, it was that King Neptune would forever protect her family and the water that they loved. But what if she and her new friends failed in their mission? Who would protect them then?

"Head toward the Davies Reef near the S.S. Yongala," Neptune said, interrupting Denise's thoughts. He gestured south with his trident. "The Diamond's thief was heading there last. And one last thing…" Neptune's electric blue eyes darkened. "Watch out for the humans. They're destroying our home, year after year, and are selfish, destructive creatures with the power to thwart your mission at every turn—intentionally or not."

King Neptune looked them all in the eye. "You *must* find the Diamond," he said. With that, Neptune struck the water with his shining golden trident and disappeared instantly back into the depths of the ocean.

As the waters settled around them, Murdock Sea Otter spoke first. "So, that's our mission."

Nicky Nautilus forced a brave smile. "That's our mission." Nodding once, briskly, she added, "And obviously we have no time to lose."

From behind some large, flaming orange coral formations, Raiden Shark grinned at his brother, Sam, and best friend, Stan.

"Well, that's convenient," he said, nodding at the departing backs of Neptune's little "team." "We know the S.S. Yongala!"

Sam and Stan burst out laughing before the three edged away from the coral. Raiden circled the others restlessly. "We've got to get that Diamond," he said, thinking out loud. His heart pounded as he thought about what the ocean could be like once the Diamond was destroyed. Neptune would no longer have power, and that would mean that he couldn't keep the oceans clean from the destruction of the humans. Eventually the waters would grow dark and Raiden would never again have to worry about his sensitive eyes tearing over painfully at light. *He'd* be the one in charge. And humans would have to enter even the shallowest waters at their own risk. Raiden circled faster and faster the more he thought about it.

"We'll get it," said Stan confidently. "And who needs Neptune, anyway?"

Raiden whirled to glare at Stan. "We don't talk about him," Raiden snapped. "His power is nothing!"

Nudging Raiden, Sam said, "C'mon. Let's not let them get too far ahead—as if that's possible."

"First, we must prepare ourselves for battle," Raiden said. "Follow me back home. That rusty heap will come in handy now," he said with a laugh as the others fell in behind him.

Back at the ship, it wasn't long before the threesome was putting the final touches on their suits of armor, turning the ragtag bits of rusted steel into fighting gear. "This will protect me from the light until the oceans are dark," Raiden said as he nodded his head to lower the shield over his eyes.

Sam grinned, showing dozens of pointy teeth that were longer and sharper than arrowheads. "Can we have some fun along the way?"

Thinking about the little puffer fish he always thrilled at chasing, Raiden laughed heartily. Sam and Stan laughed, too, and they all glided off to follow Neptune's new team.

Back at the pond, I typed Christopher Clam's story with a feeling of growing excitement. If it was true, this was definitely bigger than *Duckey Daily*. This was bigger than anything I had ever done before, and supposedly Neptune chose *me* for the job. Could it be true?

"That'll be all for tonight," Christopher Clam said, stroking his mustache thoughtfully. "You need to finish your homework…and I need to check in with the team. But believe me, Duckey, this is only the beginning."

"I told you—my name is The Duckster," I muttered. Then I helped Christopher Clam back into his bowl and opened my desk drawer so that the typewriter paper could fly in on its own. (My typewriter really was the coolest!) Christopher's words, *This is only the beginning*, echoed through my mind.

But in the middle of my happiness came a worry so sharp it made my stomach seize. If this was the real deal, what would Neptune do when he realized he'd made a mistake? What would happen when he found out he'd picked the only duck in the world afraid of water?

Chapter Three

A s the newly formed team rushed away from the meeting area, Denise Dolphin suddenly came to an abrupt halt. "Wait, guys!" she called. "What *is* this S.S. Yongala? And *where* is it? Do I need to change my outfit?"

"I've, like, never surfed there," Murdock Sea Otter replied from the wave he was riding. "That's all I can say."

"Well, of course, you haven't surfed there," Polly Puffer Fish exclaimed. "The S.S. Yongala was a huge, luxurious passenger and freight ship that sailed into the eye of a cyclone back in 1911. March 23, I believe it was. It wasn't even identified for fifty years, and it's still underwater."

Denise Dolphin, Murdock Sea Otter, Kilo Killer Whale, and Nicky Nautilus looked at Polly, mouths open.

"Polly's right," Nicky said. She curiously cocked her head to the side. "How did you know that?"

"I've got a better question!" Murdock spouted. "How did you *say* that? Up till now I thought you were someone's kid sister."

Polly blew a little bubble in reply.

"What'd she say?" Scotty Sea Gull asked in his thick accent. He dipped low and rested in the water next to Murdock's board. "This above-water thing's already getting' tiring. Mate, I reckon you're gonna have to translate some for me this journey."

Murdock raised his otter eyebrows. "But who's gonna translate what *you* say to *me*?" Everyone laughed, and despite Scotty's glares, Murdock filled him in on the S.S. Yongala.

"Ah, she's just a kid," Scotty said dismissively. "She's probably just tellin' fables."

Murdock snickered, but Denise Dolphin glared at Scotty.

"So, Polly," Denise said, swimming around in a tight circle, "where is this sunken ship? And does it have…treasure? Like…like jewelry?" Maybe the mission wouldn't be all gloom and doom, after all, Denise thought suddenly. Maybe, after they got the Diamond back, she could also find a shiny new necklace from the ship—well, it would really be a shiny *old* necklace, and it probably wouldn't be so shiny because of all the salt in the ocean…but she'd be the only blue dolphin with the only old-and-not-so-shiny necklace at Sea World! Plus she'd be partially responsible for returning Neptune's powers to him. How awesome would that be? But thinking about Neptune—and how much he needed them—instantly made Denise Dolphin feel guilty for thinking about jewelry at a time like this. She quieted and returned her gaze to Polly.

"The S.S. Yongala is near Townsville, Australia," Polly explained, more subdued. Everyone looked at her blankly. "In the Great Barrier Reef? You know, one of the Seven Wonders of the World?" Still, no one registered even a spark of recognition. Polly let out a big, dramatic sigh. "Okay, the Great Barrier Reef is the biggest coral reef system in the world. It has about three thousand individual reefs and nine hundred islands. It takes up more than one hundred and thirty thousand square miles."

"Is that bigger than Miami?" Denise asked.

After Murdock repeated the conversation—including Denise's question—to Scotty, the bird laughed and laughed.

"What?" Denise said irritably.

"I've flown over Miami," Scotty said. "If little Polly's right, the Great

Barrier Reef is almost four thousand times the size of that city. 'Is it bigger than Miami?' Please!"

Denise's turquoise eyes flashed, and Kilo Killer Whale could tell she was hurt. Before she could say anything, he jumped in with, "Well, how is she supposed to know that? She's always been at Sea World. The most talented dolphin there," he added spontaneously. Denise looked at him in surprise, and it felt like his tongue was growing bigger and bigger in his mouth. His face flushed, and he looked away.

"Okay, guys," Nicky Nautilus said calmly. "The point is that we have to get there—sooner rather than later."

"Is it a long way from here?" Kilo asked, thinking he knew the answer but wanting to shift attention away from Denise, who was still glaring at Scotty Sea Gull.

"Afraid so," Nicky said, and Polly Puffer Fish nodded energetically.

"Well, I don't know how you expect my wings to hold out for that long!" Scotty said. "I know that humans and you other beasts consider flying miraculous, but even we birds have our limits!"

"Hey!" Denise said, lifting herself out of the water as far as she could. "Let me tell you guys a little something. Coming from a showbiz family, my mom and dad and I have had to stick together, you know. The show must go on…and all of that. Well, we have a motto that I'd like to share with you guys, so listen up! *I believe…so I succeed!* We all put our fins together and say that before every show. Maybe we should do that, too. Here and now before we officially set off on our mission!" Denise waved her fins enthusiastically.

"Oh, mi-lordy" Scotty said with a roll of his eyes.

But Murdock Sea Otter spoke up quickly. "Dude, maybe she's right. I mean, we have to, like, believe in ourselves to make this thing happen, right?"

"Yeah…in fact," Kilo paused, "Neptune believes in us…so why shouldn't we believe in ourselves?"

Denise smiled and batted her eyes at Kilo. "Right!"

Scotty Sea Gull couldn't take it. "It's not that I don't believe in myself or in us, but you won't see me putting my wing in for a cheerleading session."

"I think it's kind of cool!" Murdock ruminated, stroking his whiskers.

Nicky Nautilus knew she needed to take control of the situation before a Great Debate emerged. "Let's swim for a while, and then, when we get tired…we can try out I-Zoom."

"What's I-Zoom?" Denise Dolphin asked, her interest piqued.

Nicky smiled. "We really have to get moving."

Nicky looked at the team, noticing with almost motherly pride that, despite the bickering, they all looked—well, determined. Focused. Overhead, Scotty Sea Gull was hovering impatiently, occasionally darting forward and then circling back. Denise Dolphin had turned to chat with Polly Puffer Fish, who was back to her two-word answers, while Kilo Killer Whale's eyes were trained far ahead, as if straining to see the shipwreck from here. Even Murdock Sea Otter looked antsy, hiking his baggy red shorts up and crouching low on the board. A good team, Nicky thought. Or, at least, she hoped.

"I think my wings are about to fall off!" Scotty called from above some time later.

Murdock nodded, collapsing to his belly on his board with a wet slap. "I've never surfed this hard or far in my life! It's totally…exhausting."

"Where are we?" Denise Dolphin asked, glancing around the unfamiliar deep green waters.

"We're in the Straits of Malacca," Polly Puffer Fish informed them. "Between Sumatra and Malaysia of Indonesia. Almost a third of the humans' global trade comes through here."

Scotty flew down close to the group. "That explains the hundreds of ships around us now."

Murdock shook his head, smiling. "This puffer fish dude really knows what she's talking about!"

Polly looked at him uncertainly. "Me not named Dude," she said. "Me Polly."

Kilo let out a deep belly laugh, and the others followed suit.

"I should've brought another outfit," Denise Dolphin fretted, looking for attention and glancing at the tree-lined shores on either side of the long, narrow channel. "Red totally clashes here."

"We'll be in the Pacific soon enough," Nicky reassured her, grinning. "Then you'll be fine."

Murdock opened his mouth to make a crack about Denise's wardrobe obsession, but suddenly something huge and heavy crashed down on one end of Murdock's board, sending him flying into the air in shock. Unlike when Scotty flew, however, there was nothing graceful about Murdock's airborne body.

"Duuuuuude!" Murdock shouted, catapulting back into the water. The sea surrounded him with refreshing coolness and flipped him around and around. Finally, he broke the surface, coughing and sputtering. He shook his head, disoriented, as the others rushed to his side.

Looking around, Murdock's eyes widened in disbelief. Somehow, dozens upon dozens of gigantic, drum-like containers were tumbling into the ocean from a nearby ship. Some immediately sank, making smaller fish dart away to avoid their paths, and others bobbed back up to the surface, their metallic lids glinting in the sun. Gasping and grunting, the team had to keep dodging the unpredictable onslaught. When the barrels finally stopped falling from the ship, the group huddled together, breathless and stunned.

As Murdock tried to catch his breath, one of the floating drums knocked against his board again, and he quickly read the words on the side out loud: "Warning: Radioactive Materials."

"Radio!" Denise cried out, clicking happily. "It's about time we get some real music in here! Can we take one with us? Nicky, maybe put it in your shell or something?"

Polly cut in quietly, "It's not music, Denise. The humans were probably taking these drums to the Philippines Sea, where they regularly dump tons—and I do literally mean *tons*—of trash and hazardous waste. That's what's in these drums, and when they eventually open underwater, the radioactive materials inside will kill thousands of fish and plants and

reefs…painfully." Polly's voice cracked, and she broke off.

"But that's--awful!" Denise exclaimed, trying unsuccessfully to butt away one of the heavier drums. "Stupid humans! How could they do this to our home?"

"The question is," Nicky said, "what do we do about it?"

"Look around!" Denise exclaimed. "What *can* we do?!"

Denise was right. Between the looming outlines of the ships were a thousand or more of the enormous containers, serving as a stark contrast to the things the team loved about the ocean—the clear swirling waters, the shockingly vibrant colors, the miraculous and peaceful way no one questioned *how* to live, but just lived. The ugly, dangerous containers were completely blocking the team's path through the narrow straits. No one but Polly Puffer Fish or Nicky Nautilus would even be able to get through without moving them—Kilo Killer Whale was already surrounded on all sides--and turning around would lose days of time. That was not an option, Nicky knew.

"Polly?" Denise Dolphin pressed. "What do we do next?"

With half a dozen pairs of eyes staring intently at her, Polly fell silent. Then she exclaimed, "Me not know!"

"Aaaaand she's back!" Scotty said dryly.

"Look, guys—we have to move them, pick them up somehow," Nicky Nautilus said. "We just don't have any other choice."

"The problem is," Kilo cut in, "even if we could get all the drums together, where would we put them?"

They all exchanged dumbfounded glances. Then Kilo had an idea. "We could dump them back onto the ship they came from."

"Yes!" Denise Dolphin seconded the thought. "Teach them a lesson."

The team glanced at one another, their faces radiating determination, excitement, and maybe a little fear. They had never done anything like this before.

Kilo, with his huge tailfin, began trying to sweep the drums toward one common point. Everyone chipped in with what they could. Denise Dolphin determinedly butted one drum at a time toward the ship with her nose, Murdock Sea Otter and Scotty Sea Gull began pushing the floating drums, and Nicky Nautilus and Polly Puffer Fish tried to heave what they could to where Kilo was guiding the trash. But the fact of the matter was that five out of six of them—even *with* a killer whale—were just too small to make any difference. The waves kept knocking the huge barrels together and then apart, sending them scattering like oversized marbles. And the passageway was still too jam-packed to swim through.

"There's gotta be a better way to do this!" Scotty Sea Gull called, frustrated.

Polly kept trying to push the drums with all of her strength, but she couldn't stop blowing anxious, angry bubbles. Then, all of a sudden, one of her bubbles shot from her body with amazing speed and strength, knocking half a dozen barrels aside and sending other fish dashing away in alarm as the barrels careened across the ocean.

Nicky looked at her, astonished. "Polly!"

"Me do?" Polly asked, her eyes wide.

"Yes! I don't know how you did it, but that's perfect! You can use that super-bubble to help propel the drums together!" Nicky's eyes were bright with renewed hope.

Polly slowly shook her body from side to side, looking at the endless stretch of barrels surrounding them. She couldn't move those gigantic, heavy things. The bubble was a one-time thing; she'd never done anything like that before in her life!

"You have to do this, Polly," Kilo said firmly, "so that we can find the Diamond in time to help Neptune."

Polly looked at her new friends. They were all counting on her. No one had ever counted on her before, and her body felt swollen with pride and fear. "Okay," Polly said softly.

With encouraging smiles, Kilo, Denise, Nicky, and Murdock moved out of her way, and Scotty watched from above, mildly skeptical. Closing her eyes, Polly concentrated with all her might, trying to focus on how angry she was at the humans for polluting their home without a second thought, without guilt or regret—but all she could do was blow normal bubbles. Normal dumb bubbles that popped as soon as they made contact with the drums beside them! She blew and blew until she felt she was about to pass out from exhaustion—but not one bubble was even strong enough to push a minnow aside, let alone a thousand huge, heavy drums full of poison.

Denise groaned impatiently. "It's not working! We don't have time for this."

Polly looked guiltily at the team, her body expanding in embarrassment. She was about to apologize when Nicky Nautilus, looking behind

Polly Puffer Fish, exclaimed, "Wait! I have an idea! I'll be right back—hopefully with help!"

Nicky darted past Polly, and the others looked after her in confusion. Nicky was heading toward a veritable cloud of starfish and seahorses, which was edging closer from a distance.

"Where is she going?" Murdock asked rhetorically. No one answered; everyone was too busy watching Nicky and trying to hear what she was saying.

Finally, Nicky returned, with the starfish and seahorses following close behind, one big starfish in the lead.

"Um," Scotty Sea Gull cracked, nodding at the unlikely army. "Who ordered the crustaceans on horseback?"

Ignoring him, Nicky grinned triumphantly. "These are the Samurai Starfish and Seahorses. Neptune saved their home once, the coral atolls of the Ryuku island chain," she explained. When the others just stared, she exhaled impatiently. "It's off the coast of Okinawa, Japan. Anyway, they owe him, so even though they're peaceful kelp farmers, they'll help us—and they have a plan." She bowed to the lead starfish, which bowed back. "And that's their Sensei," Nicky added.

"Sensei?" Murdock asked.

"Their leader," said Nicky Nautilus.

"How do you understand them?" Kilo pressed.

Nicky blushed. "I speak and understand all the languages of the oceans. But that's not important right now. We all need to work together. Watch!"

In what sounded like gibberish to everyone but Nicky, the Sensei began issuing orders to the other starfish and seahorses, who all spread out, looking determined and purposeful. Then they all linked together to form one brilliant net under the hundreds of barrels. The Sensei motioned to Nicky, who shouted to the team in response, "Come on, guys, push all the drums into the net!"

Struggling against the current, Kilo pushed the drums with his tail, while Denise again nudged them forward with her nose. Nicky pulled out an oversized paddle from her shell and began shoving the drums forward, while Polly, Scotty, and Murdock teamed up to urge the lighter, floating ones toward the starfish net. The huge net cupped inwards, capturing as many barrels as it could. Then the Sensei bowed to Kilo Killer Whale, and he suddenly understood that they needed his help. He jetted off to push more drums in their direction with his enormous fins, circling around and pushing the barrels until the waters were clear again. When all of the drums were aligned above the net, Denise Dolphin gasped, an idea hitting, and impulsively dove down below and began spinning counterclockwise. Her motions created a waterspout under the net that sent the drums flying into the air—and onto the humans' ship. (Most of the starfish and seahorses got the ride of their lives, too, yelling "Bonsai!!!" on their way up.)

From the surface, Murdock and Scotty let out whoops of disbelief. The barge rocked and shuddered as hundreds of drums cascaded onto the deck, and the humans shouted out in surprise.

From his surfboard, Murdock watched the humans look at each other in shock, not understanding what was happening.

Murdock couldn't resist: Thinking of how horribly awry the humans could have made the mission go with their carelessness, he paddled just a *little* closer to the ship, cupped his hands around his mouth, and called in his most haunting voice, "*From the sea itself! No more dumping!*"

As the men kept looking to the silent water for answers, Murdock rejoined the rest of the team with a victorious smile.

"Impressive," Scotty said from above. "Where, might I ask, did you pick up the English?"

"Ah, just one of the perks of hangin' out with the surfers in California!"

"Whooey!" Denise cried, oblivious to Murdock but unable to dampen her own enthusiasm. "Did you all see that? That was the best trick I've ever done! Ever!"

"That was, indeed, sick," Murdock said, grinning widely. The tone of his voice made it clear that it was a compliment.

Nicky, too, laughed in delight, waving at the departing samurai starfish and seahorses. "Girl, that was just about the coolest thing I've ever

seen!"

"Just about?" Denise Dolphin countered, pretending to be insulted. She playfully swatted Nicky. "Don't be shy; you can say it. That was awesome! I was awesome!"

Kilo was amazed. He wanted to tell her how heroic and quick-thinking she had been, but his tongue seemed too dry in his mouth. (Ironic, with all the water around.) All he could do was cough a lame, "Uh, yeah. Wow, Denise."

Polly was the only one who was silent, but, in the middle of their celebration, nobody else even noticed.

"Neptune!" Nicky cried suddenly. "We should check in with Neptune before we get moving again." She pulled the huge, ornate gold mirror from her shell, and everyone gathered around her, excited to tell Neptune of their first adventure and success. But when Neptune's face appeared in the mirror, the team exchanged alarmed glances. Their great ruler's eyes were deeply shadowed, his golden-red hair and beard no longer glowing.

"King Neptune—" Nicky started, but Neptune interrupted.

"My strength is weakening so quickly. You *must* find that Diamond."

"I know, but—" Nicky tried to explain.

"Forget about everything else!" Neptune snapped. "Without the Diamond, nothing else matters."

Nicky swallowed past a lump in her throat as Neptune's image faded, and she slipped the mirror back in her shell without a word.

"Well, you heard him," Scotty said. "Let's get a move on. We have to almost be there, right?"

Polly shook her head grimly, not looking at anyone, and the team finally began weaving their way through the Straits of Malacca.

Raiden, Sam, and Stan were already more than half a day's swim ahead of Neptune's ragtag bunch. Looking behind him pointlessly, Raiden laughed. "So, how much do you think those barrels set them back?"

"A brilliant maneuver, bro," Sam said, nodding appreciatively. "I never would have thought of that."

Stan grinned. "Definitely. I mean, the humans would have dumped 'em eventually, but this way, Neptune's little team is probably still trying to shove that whale through the cracks! Can't you just see it now? I wish I could take a picture."

The three practically convulsed with laughter, scaring schools of fish away instantly. It was good being the undisputed terrors of the ocean.

Chapter four

the team had been swimming for less than an hour when Murdock Sea Otter called from his board, "Hey, dudes? Nicky? What would you think about using that I-Zoom thing right now—whatever that is? We're all tired and we lost some time back there."

Nicky Nautilus chewed her lip thoughtfully. "I don't know…"

"Yeah, c'mon, Nicky," Scotty Sea Gull called irritably. "It's all well and good in the water where there's no gravity, but these wings have been holding my weight for days now. I could use a break."

"I'm glad you're feeling the team spirit," Denise Dolphin said, teasing him.

Remembering the urgency in Neptune's eyes, Nicky finally nodded. "Okay, you guys are right. Here's how it works. I just have to focus on our destination, the Davies Reef, and think of something that makes me feel a powerful emotion. Joy, excitement, anger—"

"Terror?" Polly Puffer Fish blurted.

Nicky smiled kindly. "Sure, Polly. Even terror. That emotion, blended with the focus on the Davies Reef, basically acts like gasoline—and it transports me almost wherever I want to go. How do you think I got to you all—spread out around the world—in one day?"

The team exchanged glances, flabbergasted.

"But—where do you get the power from?" Denise asked.

Nicky looked evasive. "I've just always had it. Anyway, I've never actually used it with anyone else, so here's the catch…you all have to jump into my shell."

Kilo Killer Whale looked at Nicky, who was tinier than his eyeball, and burst out laughing. "You're a great salesman, Nicky. You said that with such a straight face."

Denise started giggling, too. "Can you imagine?" She mimed leaping into Nicky's shell, and everybody laughed along but Nicky.

"Look, do you guys want to just keep swimming till you pass out, or do you want to try it?" Nicky asked irritably. She pulled her head and torso back into her shell and, as if from a cavernous depth, called, "One at time—jump in!"

Kilo, Denise, Polly, Murdock, and Scotty looked at one another doubtfully.

"You're kidding, right?" Scotty asked. "No way! You can all just go ahead and *succeed* without your feathered friend!"

"Me try," Polly exclaimed. Nodding at everyone else, she swam straight toward the tiny opening in Nicky's shell, and even though she was afraid to just crash into her friend, she didn't swerve; and then, quite suddenly, Polly was inside a huge, dark, warehouse-like structure. Gasping, she outstretched a fin and touched one of the "walls," and it was smooth and warm like a—well, like a shell.

"It's a little messy," came a small voice. "But then, I don't usually have visitors in here."

It took Polly a second to realize that the voice was Nicky's, and another to see Nicky blinking self-consciously at Polly from several feet away.

"How—how?" was all Polly could say before she was interrupted by a high-pitched yell and a streak of blue against the inky darkness. Denise Dolphin!

"What in the world…?" Denise asked breathlessly, getting her bearings. She looked around and finally saw Polly and Nicky, just specks in the enormous cavity.

Then, slipping and sliding, came Murdock, clutching his board. Scotty, squawking indignantly, was still squirming to get loose from Murdock's clutches. "What the…? Well, I'll be a… It worked!" the soaking wet seagull said. They were only missing…

"Kilo!" everyone shouted as, with a noise like a cork popping, the killer whale flew through the entrance of Nicky's shell, colliding with the back wall. Strangely, it seemed like the shell was constantly shifting, growing to accommodate the new arrivals.

With some shuffling and disbelieving laughter, the group finally got its bearings and turned to face Nicky.

"Welcome to my home," she said graciously.

Murdock Sea Otter peered at the rows and rows of shelves lining the shell's outer walls. On them, neatly labeled, was everything from human double-A batteries to a battered xylophone. "You're quite the collector, aren't you?" Murdock asked, reaching for a pair of neon swim trunks that caught his eye.

Nicky slapped his hand. "I don't go rooting around your home, do I?" she chided. "And, no, I'm not a collector. I'm a *keeper of things*. It's different."

Nicky's face looked more vulnerable than anyone had ever seen it, and Kilo suddenly wondered if she ever got lonely, all alone in this big shell.

"Anyway, since we're all in here, I think it's best if we *all* focus on the Davies Reef and a powerful emotion," Nicky said brusquely. She grabbed hold of one of the shelves, as though bracing herself. "Okay—you all ready?"

Everyone exchanged heady, excited glances and nodded, closing their eyes. It didn't take much urging for Kilo to think of his family, wondering what they were doing and whether they missed him. Suddenly, almost without realizing it, he was thrust into I-Zoom, a strange combination of pressure and noise and silence with only the occasional rattling

of one of Nicky's stored objects interrupting the quiet. He couldn't see the others, but the pressure around him was comforting, and he knew they were there.

Then, just as abruptly, he was sucked back into the ocean and could see again, and he felt like he'd just had the air knocked out of him.

One by one, the other members of the team popped up around him, their eyes bright with adrenaline.

"Wow!" Denise said, straightening her blouse. "That was nuts! How long did that last?"

Nicky just smiled. "It was the work of a moment." She looked around at the blank faces and then said, "It doesn't matter. We're here. We're together. We're on a mission." Let's just hope it's even faster next time."

"Why's that?" Murdock asked.

Nicky widened her eyes in exasperation. "You guys are *heavy!* You think little flying Scotty's got it bad--how long do you think I can carry you without getting tired?"

Kilo Killer Whale ducked his head sheepishly. "Sorry."

"Well, that was the weirdest *moment* of my life!" Scotty said, flapping his wings to dry off as he bobbed on the ripples of ocean.

"No kiddin', dude!" Murdock chimed in, back on his board. The others laughed, agreeing.

"And we did it together," cheered Denise.

"Maybe we should call it We-Zoom," said Nicky.

A faint blush crept up Nicky's neck, and Denise sensed it wasn't often that Nicky Nautilus had a "we."

"Well, it does seem to be working out that way, doesn't it?" Scotty Sea Gull offered.

"I think that's perfect," Denise said, flashing Nicky a bright grin.

After a moment of companionable silence, Murdock glanced around the rippling, open sea. There was no shore to be seen on any side. "So... where are we?"

Everyone looked at Polly, and she blushed. "We're in the Philippines Sea—which was probably where the ship with the radioactive barrels was heading. Since it's so far from land, humans come here often to dump their trash."

Denise asked angrily, "Don't they know others live here?"

"They choose to dump in the oceans over burying their trash and hazardous waste on land," Polly explained softly. "Maybe it seems like the lesser of two evils, so to speak."

"Yeah, well—it's not!" Denise sputtered. After a second, her face brightened. "Hey, guys, remember how awesome my waterspout was?"

Four seas and countless islands later, Denise still couldn't seem to stop talking about her save-the-day moment. At first, the rest of the team was just as happy to reenact the scene…but now Murdock Sea Otter wished he could just jump on the next wave and ride it far away from the chattering dolphin. *But we're a team,* he thought, a little grimly, for the thousandth time since yesterday. *We've gotta stick together.*

With Scotty flying overhead and Murdock coasting along on his board, the rest of the group swam in a straight line next to each other. That was the great thing about the ocean; it was so huge, so unknowably vast, that no one was forced to swim behind anyone else or, worse, crunched into someone's body. Back home, Murdock couldn't understand how the other otters would sun themselves practically one on top of the other. Gross. He just wanted to say to his family and their neighbors, "There's room for everybody!"

"I can just about see the Great Barrier Reef!" Scotty called from overhead. He squinted and dipped down low to the ocean.

"Really?" Denise squealed. "We're almost there?"

Scotty laughed. "No."

"No?" Denise echoed, confused. "Did I miss something?"

Murdock shot the bird a dirty look. "He's just messing with us," he said. "Aren't you, man?"

Scotty dipped and pecked Murdock's shoulder. "Well, can you blame me? It's getting a bit old, hearing about our heroine's second of glory. It would seem our starlet is more concerned with her own success than our mission's success!"

Kilo Killer Whale jumped in. "If it were any one of us, we'd want to keep talking about it, too."

Everyone looked at him, and he hedged.

"Ohh," Scotty said. "Isn't that cute? The whale and the dolphin, sitting in a tree—"

The group's banter faded to Polly as she slowly fell behind. She wished that once, just once, she could do something as important and extraordinary as what Denise had done. She wanted to show the team that she was more than just a silly little puffer fish, the dumb little tag-along. She could do things, too. Couldn't she?

Polly was so lost in her thoughts that she jerked in surprise when someone called, "Over here!" At first, she thought it was one of her friends, but she didn't recognize the voice. She whirled around, thinking she was hearing things.

"Hello?" she called. No response. She called out a little louder. "Hel-lo?"

There was a muffled cry, and then the voice came again. "Over here! Help, I'm all caught up!"

Finally, Polly realized that it wasn't anyone she knew calling out at all. Her gaze landed on a little angelfish, even tinier than she was, its bright orange and blue body tangled in a spool of fishing wire.

Uh, oh.

Polly got as close to the little fish as she could, staring hard at the wire. It was wrapped around the angelfish several dozen times, pinning her fins to her sides as she struggled against it.

"Helloooo?" the angelfish said. "Are you going to help me or what?" She looked at Polly urgently. "I've been here for hours, and I'm *so* tired."

Polly looked around, scanning desperately for one of the others. Nicky Nautilus would have something to cut the wire. But there was no one in sight. "Oh—but—but—me not know how."

Then Polly had an idea. The bubbles! She glanced around again, this time to make sure she really was the only member of the team in the area. She didn't want anyone seeing if she messed up again.

"Okay," she said. "Me try something. Bubble push—break fishing line."

The angelfish looked at her blankly.

Polly closed her eyes and concentrated, remembering her one super-sonic bubble and how it had sped across the ocean floor like the bowling ball she'd seen some bigger fish play with once. *Try,* she thought, and the air filled her body until she couldn't hold it in for another millisecond.

She opened her mouth and then her eyes to see a perfect little bubble shoot out toward the angelfish.

It popped as soon as it touched the fishing line, and Polly almost burst into tears of disappointment.

"Me sorry," Polly managed, hardly even able to look at the angelfish.

"Do it again," the angelfish implored. "Please?"

Her eyes were big with hope, like Polly was her last chance in the world, and all of a sudden, without even thinking about it, a bubble flew out of Polly and slammed into the angelfish, instantly snapping the plastic fishing line and sending the fish flying across the ocean. Polly gasped in delight.

"Aaiigh!" the angelfish yelled in surprise. "Thank youuu!"

Polly had already lost sight of the fish, but she called back happily, "You're welcome!"

Another voice, this time unmistakably Kilo's, cried out, "Polly! Over here!" She raced toward his voice, feeling like she could do anything. She couldn't wait to tell the others what she had done!

But when she caught up to them, Kilo just stared at her reprovingly. "Polly, you can't separate from the rest of us. It costs us more time."

Polly's eyes widened. "But—but me—" But the more she tried to tell the story, the more she stumbled on her words, until finally, with the team's eyes on her, she simply quieted and kept swimming.

"Hey, Polly?" Scotty Sea Gull called later that evening. "Where are we? I think I'm starting to see land."

"Don't listen to him, Polly. He's just messing with you," Murdock Sea Otter said tiredly. Lying on his stomach on the board, with the water moving so gently, he could hardly keep his head up.

"No, really," Scotty argued. "Trust me. I've got a pretty good view from up here."

"We're off the coast of Papua New Guinea," Polly said quietly. She wasn't much in a talking mood.

Denise Dolphin, however, made up for it. "We are *unstoppable!*" she chattered. "We've got We-Zoom, Polly's practically got a built-in navigation system—and, of course, my waterspout..."

The whole team, including Kilo Killer Whale, groaned. Right now, he'd much rather listen to little Polly tell them where they were. He didn't recognize these waters or many of the kinds of fish swimming by them. Despite traveling all over the world with his pod, it never stopped amazing him just how big the ocean was.

He started to turn back to Denise Dolphin, surprised that she'd cut herself off. Then she let out a high-pitched shriek that made his body go cold. "Denise!" he exclaimed. "What's wrong?"

As soon as the words were out of his mouth, he knew the answer. In the middle of reenacting her waterspout action, Denise had swum straight into a net, and Nicky Nautilus had gotten stuck with her. The openings between the ropes were so small that even Nicky couldn't squeeze through. Denise struggled and thrashed desperately, and her eyes, wide with fear for the first time since he'd known her, met with Kilo's.

"Help!" she screamed, as the net slowly, slowly began rising to the surface.

"Aw, you've gotta be kidding me!" called Murdock in disbelief.

"Let me see, let me see," Nicky said to herself, disappearing frantically into her shell. "Scissors, I have to have scissors. Or glass. Or a sharp rock."

"Something!" Denise cried. "Oh, please, find something!" She gasped in panic. The thought of being caught by humans and never being able to see her parents or Sea World or her friends again was making her heart ache. What would the humans do to her up there once they got her on the boat?

Polly flitted around the net helplessly. "What do? What do?"

Kilo wasn't about to wait for Nicky to find a random blade in her shell. How dare the humans?! After everything else they'd done to the oceans, they were *not* going to take his friends, too! Setting his jaw, he focused on the boat, which was much smaller than the icebergs he used to send hurling across the surface. Restraining his anger as much as he could, he swam straight toward the boat, ramming it hard.

"Hey!" cried one of the humans above. "What the—!"

"Ouch!" Denise cried, as the net swung wildly and slammed against the boat's side.

Coming from the other side, Kilo shoved the boat again. And again. And again. The people on board, as well as Denise and Nicky, were crying out in grunts as they tried to simply grab hold of something. Finally, with one final push, the net snapped off the boat, and Denise wriggled hysterically, trying to get out.

"Wait!" Kilo said. "You'll get tangled. Polly, help me."

Polly Puffer Fish hadn't realized her spikes had thrust out, but she hooked them under one end of the net and lifted, creating an opening for Denise, Nicky, and dozens of other small fish to cascade out. Finally free, Denise Dolphin shuddered, so upset she was nearly hyperventilating.

"It's okay," Kilo soothed, coming closer to her. "You're okay now."

Her eyes flashed. "You didn't have to rock the boat so hard, you know! That hurt!" She turned her back to him, and Kilo flinched.

"Hey," Kilo started to say, feeling hurt. "What about our motto? I was trying to..."

"Whatever!" Denise retorted.

"Denise," Nicky Nautilus said in a low voice, locking eyes with Kilo. "That's no way to say thank you. Thank you," she said louder to Kilo, offering him a shaky smile.

Denise didn't mean to sound ungrateful. She was just so embarrassed! Her stupid showing off had nearly cost her and Nicky their lives! She sniffed, trying hard not to cry. To escape her friends' gazes, she forced herself up through the water, leaping high and catching Scotty Sea Gull's relieved eyes. Great. Everyone felt sorry for her. And now it was starting to rain!

"Ugh," she said, plunging back into the ocean and shaking off the rainwater, trying to sound like she hadn't been fighting back tears. "I got wet! Now I'll have to change my blouse!"

The others exchanged amused glances. "Um, Denise?" Murdock Sea Otter asked carefully. "You know you're already wet...right? You know, like, we all are?"

Denise huffed. "Yeah, with *salt* water! That was fresh water up there! It's different...it's just not the same...it's weird...I need to change. Nicky?"

"Yep, on it," Nicky said, crawling back in her shell. She scuffled around and finally emerged with a bright pink, silky blouse. "Will this do?"

"Yes," Denise said, cheering up. "That's pretty. Thank you!"

Murdock and Kilo shrugged, and Nicky retreated coyly back into her shell.

Grinning at the team and raising one chubby finger to his mouth, Murdock edged closer to Nicky, slowly lowering his head until one eye was pressed against the shell. He squinted, silently urging his eye to adjust to the cavernous darkness—and hoping he wouldn't fall in by mistake! Then, all of a sudden, Nicky's little head popped up, startling him like the Jack-in-the-Box he'd found near the California shore—and nearly poking his eye.

"Hey! Do I go spying around *your* domicile?" Nicky asked defensively.

Murdock let out a gurgling laugh. "You wouldn't find much there, except a bunch of sweaty otters."

Nicky wrinkled her nose, but she still looked protective. "Like I said earlier, I'm a keeper of things. Throughout all of my travels, I gather and store things that I might need later."

After a moment of silence, Scotty Sea Gull said, "Well, you might want to pick up some scissors later. Just in case."

"I'll *keep* that in mind," she quipped dryly. "Come on, everyone. We've still got a ways to go."

Chapter five

"Can you pass the broccoli?" I asked, reaching across the dinner table for the vegetable bowl (which looked pretty similar to Christopher Clam's bowl). Mom smiled as she held it out to me.

"You're such a dork," said my older brother, Danny. He shook his head, grinning at Deb conspiratorially. "You like broccoli—*and* you're afraid of water!"

"Liking broccoli isn't weird!" Deb defended me, reaching for the bowl. "I like it, too."

"Well, how about a duck being scared of water? That's weird. What are you, a cat in disguise?" Danny asked me. He held the tips of his wings up to his face like whiskers. "Meeeeow."

"Alright," Dad said sternly. "That's enough."

"Dad, I don't need you to stick up for me," I snapped, feeling heat rise under my feathers. "I'm not a little kid. I've got my adult feathers, you know."

I looked at my plate. I could feel the heat of everyone's gazes and the meaning behind them—Mom, Dad, and Deb's sympathy and Danny's taunting. It wasn't fair. Whenever Deb was the center of attention, it was because she came home with yet another trophy. Danny drew people to him with his easy confidence. But me, well…there was always something I couldn't do, it seemed. I sighed. "I'm not hungry anymore. I'm going to my room."

Mom and Dad exchanged glances.

"Okay, honey," Mom said after a hesitation, glaring at Danny.

"Sorry, Duckey," Danny said dutifully. He snickered, but I ignored his amused grin as I pulled away from the table.

Our old wooden boathouse smelled warm and oaky as I took my plate to the kitchen. We'd lived there for as long as I could remember, making our home among the half disintegrated oars and bottles of spilled sun cream that we made the mistake of tasting as hatchlings. Humans probably wouldn't think our place was so pretty, but it was the best home I could imagine.

After washing my plate and putting it away, I retreated to my room and leaned against the wall for a second. It was soft with years of rain and (thankfully) human neglect, and the coolness of it against my back always relaxed me. Angry at letting Danny's teasing get to me, I shook my head and pulled a book from my shelf. *Moby Dick.* Mom had read the book to us years ago when we three ducklings clamored for the privilege of snuggling against her. Deb and Danny always fell asleep right away, but I forced my heavy eyes to stay open, imagining Ishmael's adventures onboard Captain Ahab's ship. Mom always read the book with such energy, letting her voice rise and fall like waves with the flow of the story. Now, of course, I couldn't look at it the same way. Even though Moby Dick wasn't a killer whale, like Kilo, I just couldn't bear the thought of anyone hunting either of them down. I closed the book and set it on my nightstand.

Someone rapped lightly on the door, and Dad came in with a little plate of ice cream. He came and sat next to me on the bed.

"Dad," I grumbled. "What did I say? I'm not a little kid anymore—I don't need ice cream to make me feel better."

"Who said it was for you?" Dad retorted, swallowing a big spoonful. He leaned in closer to me. "Look, Duckey. There's something I want to tell you."

"My name is The Duckster, Dad," I insisted, for the millionth time.

Dad set the plate on his lap and put another spoonful of ice cream into his mouth. Clearly the dessert was never meant for me at all.

"It's about Neptune...and how I know him," Dad said, looking at me seriously.

"Okay..." I raised my eyebrows only slightly, hoping to look aloof. But before I knew it, I was caught by his story; ensnared.

When Dad was only a hatchling, he said, he used to "belong" to a little girl he only dimly remembered now. He was traveling with the girl and her family on a cruise ship bigger and grander than most buildings, all shiny and white, and she had to hide him, because animals weren't allowed on board. Dad and the little girl would play in secret; only her parents knew. He was having a great time, he said, and had the run of the family's suite, which seemed enormous to him. Then, one night, the ship began to rock violently, like enormous hands were shaking it in anger. The room lit up with lightning, and the crashing thunder made him burrow into the little girl's neck. It was Dad's first storm, and it was a bad one.

Soon, Dad's sensitive new ears rang with a sharp, shrill noise over the intercom, which made the little girl start to cry in fear. "Let's go," her parents said, reaching for the little girl's hands and strapping a puffy vest to her chest. She only let them take one hand, though, because the other was tightly clutching Dad. Together, the four of them joined a mass of terrified people streaming down the hall and down the stairs. A disembodied voice encouraged everyone to stay calm, but the voice cracked, not inspiring confidence. At one point, the shuddering ship slammed the little girl against a wall, and she almost dropped Dad.

Finally, the family gathered around a door of the ship where crew-members were hurriedly rushing people into lifeboats. Dad said the girl's mother was egg-white as she climbed down the ladder, looking up at her husband. The wind threw sheets of water at the little girl, who coughed and sputtered, and her dad lifted her over the side to pass her to a crewmember. At that moment, a massive wave hurled against the side of the ship, making the metal and wood crack under its force. The little girl screamed a high-pitched, vibrating wail, and she tried to grab hold of the railing, eyes open wide in terror. Her father yelled and reached for her but was thrown back with another wave, and the little girl—with my Dad tucked in her hand—fell down, down, down into the swirling, angry waters.

The water slapped Dad hard, nearly knocking him out, and snatched him from the little girl's hand. The waves pulled him under, then threw him up into their frothy swells, only to suck him back down again, making Dad so dizzy and disoriented he couldn't even be scared. All he could think of was the little girl. Then, right as Dad's vision was blackening, a huge hand rose up from the water and pulled him out! Trying to open his eyes against the sting of saltwater and rainwater in his face, Dad barely made out another hand holding the coughing little girl, whose soaked hair covered her face like a web. The hand lifted her above the lifeboats and gently laid her next to her sobbing parents. The next thing Dad knew, he was waking up, terrified, in the deepest, darkest part of the ocean—except, he could breathe! And there, waiting for him to wake up, was a figure he would later know as King Neptune.

"I was telling your mom the story one night," Dad concluded, finishing the ice cream, "and I didn't realize you had come into the kitchen until you started crying. You'd heard everything, Duckster. And you couldn't sleep for weeks with nightmares."

I looked at him like he was speaking another language. "But I don't remember that at all."

"Well, a part of you does," Dad said. "See…your fear of water—it's not your fault. It's mine."

I didn't know how to feel or what to say, so, for the first time in my life, *I* comforted *Dad* by wrapping my wings around him and holding tight.

I tossed and turned in bed that night. All I could think of was Dad and Neptune and the ocean…and me. Why me? If these stories were real, why did Neptune choose me? What did all of this mean? I sat up in bed,

and the light from the full moon hit me in the face. I always loved how
the moon looked on the water, and before I knew it, there I was, standing at the edge of the pond. I took a deep breath…and waded out into
the darkness, watching the water inch up my short legs. When I looked
up, I saw the reflection of the moon on the water. It made a trail that
started at my feet and stretched all of the way across the pond. *Could I
believe? Could I succeed?* I never realized how big the pond was until that

moment, and I thought about the vast ocean beyond. I gulped and stood there for a long, long time.

Meanwhile, in the deepest, quietest part of the ocean, King Neptune was touching the tall cradle where the Diamond once rested. It was strange; the Diamond had been there for so long that he'd almost stopped noticing it. The glowing, beautiful stone had simply become a part of his palace, a decoration of sorts. Neptune shook his head angrily. How could he have been so stupid? So arrogant as to believe the Diamond needed him more than he needed it?

Now, without the Diamond, he was of little good to the oceans and creatures he so loved. He raised his hands to his face, turning them over to look at the new age spots that had developed seemingly overnight. His hands looked smaller somehow, so much less powerful than they'd always been.

"*Aaaaggghhh!*" Neptune roared suddenly, overcome by his feeling of helplessness. Closing his eyes, he gripped his trident and yelled again, trying to loosen the tightness in his chest. With mouths puckered in fright, a school of small fish streamed out of Neptune's palace, taking only parting glances at their leader.

It took Neptune a second to realize that the deep rumbling all around him was not caused by his frustrated, furious cry. It was separate from him entirely, and the ocean floor began to shake violently, loosening coral formations and distressing the palace walls. Neptune put his hands to the walls in disbelief, as if trying to hold the palace steady while the tremors intensified into a powerful earthquake. Realizing the inevitable, Neptune had no choice but to escape, and from a short distance away, he watched with his hands clenched into fists at his sides as the earthquake ripped the palace from the ground on which it had been built millennia ago. With nothing holding it together, the palace crumbled into enormous, sharp fragments of rock, many of which disintegrated into sand that simply drifted away. In minutes, what had been the most glorious structure in the world was unrecognizable—nothing more than floating seaweed and coral, reef and stone. Neptune, standing in the middle of the open ocean floor, was unable to look away from the *nothing* that had once been his home.

The ground gave one final, slow shudder, and three small, dark creatures in heavy construction gear poked their heads up from the new cracks. The first creature crawled out sheepishly, and the others followed until they faced Neptune in a tight semicircle. Their sensitive, pointed ears wriggled at the inaudible vibrations still coming from the ocean floor, and they reluctantly met Neptune's fiery eyes with their own guilty, almond-shaped ones.

"Uh, oh," the first creature said, looking around. "Did we do this?"

Neptune glared at the Subterranean Guys. Rarely seen, their job was to balance the earth's plates by causing tiny, unrecorded tremors—*not* earthquakes strong enough to destroy the oldest, most important formation in the ocean! "Yes!" Neptune roared, throwing his arms open to indicate all that the Subterranean Guys had ruined.

"I told you we'd gone too far!" the first Subterranean Guy exclaimed, poking the comrade to his left.

"You did not!" the comrade sputtered indignantly, poking the first one back. "It's his fault! He was in the lead—Mr. 'I can see perfectly in pitch dark'!" He pointed to the Subterranean Guy at the far end of the semicircle, who shook his head vehemently.

Instantly, they all began bickering, turning their backs on King Neptune and poking each other in the shoulders, pointing down at the cracks and then around at the damage. Neptune cleared his throat pointedly, still flushed with rage.

"Oh—erm—sorry about that," said the first Subterranean Guy. He leaned forward conspiratorially to King Neptune, casting a quick look at the others. "These guys—they don't know what they're doing."

"Enough!" Neptune yelled, slamming his trident into to the ground. The Subterranean Guys quieted, and Neptune leveled his gaze on the second one. "What did you say about pitch dark?" he asked.

The third Subterranean Guy looked at the others, as if for permission to speak, and they shoved him forward until he was standing directly

before King Neptune. "Thanks a lot," he muttered behind him, and the others snickered. Then, looking at Neptune, he said quickly, "We're used to the dark. You know that. But this—" he gestured widely, his thick construction glove almost flying off, "—this is something else entirely. It's hard enough to see each other down there, let alone anything else. We thought we were a thousand miles away from here!"

The other Subterranean Guys all began to speak at once.

"It's true!"

"He's right!"

"Can't see the hammers in front of our faces!"

King Neptune looked around, dread making his body go cold, then hot. The Subterranean Guys were right. The ocean was much darker than it had been even yesterday, a deep, inky blue that made the water seem endless and the surface only a myth. Neptune had been so closed up in his palace that he hadn't realized, hadn't made the connection…

"We'll build you another palace!" the first Subterranean Guy burst out, misinterpreting Neptune's stony silence.

"Yeah!" said the second, nodding enthusiastically. "We build underwater caves and caverns every day! We can do that!"

"The only thing is…" the third added.

Neptune raised his eyebrows as the Subterranean Guys lowered their heads together and began speaking over each other.

"The only thing is…" Neptune prompted impatiently.

The first Subterranean Guy coughed awkwardly. "Well…it's too dark. We can't see what we're doing. Obviously."

The second Subterranean Guy elbowed him. "Unless…" He motioned to the one next to him, who reached into his pocked and pulled out a shard of crystal, about six inches long. It caught the little light remaining in the ocean and tossed it around in brilliant pinks and blues and greens. "Unless we build it of crystal. Entirely of crystal."

Warming to the idea, the others exploded into a chorus of agreement. Neptune thought about it. A crystal palace, lighting up the oceans. Letting everyone know that he was here, to care for and protect them. *Yes,* he thought. It felt right.

"Just get it done," Neptune said finally, feeling weak.

"We know of a place," said the first Subterranean Guy, "that's rich with beautiful crystals. We can build it there. It'll be—"

"No," Neptune interrupted. His gaze flickered briefly to the Diamond's cradle, the only part of the palace still standing. "It has to be here. And soon."

As the Subterranean Guys burrowed back below the ocean floor, with promises to return shortly with the crystal, Neptune glided toward the cradle. Placing a hand on its surface, he tried to call Nicky through the mirror—but it was no use. As he'd suspected, the last of his communication with the team had disappeared with his palace.

Chapter Six

Kilo Killer Whale had never seen the group this quiet. Denise Dolphin had hardly said a word since the net incident, Polly Puffer Fish seemed to have gone totally mute, Nicky Nautilus's jaw was clenched tight as she swam, and even fun-loving Murdock Sea Otter and snarky Scotty Sea Gull seemed too immersed in the task of moving forward to make conversation. But Kilo didn't mind. It gave him space to think.

It had occurred to him awhile back that Neptune had never revealed *why* the Diamond had been stolen, or even given the team a hint as to whom they were searching for. So what if they managed to make it to the Davies Reef in one piece? They didn't have a clue what to look for once they got there. There had to be thousands and thousands of fish that made their home in that area. What did the team expect—that the thief would be wearing the Diamond around its neck with a sign that read, *I'm right here!* No. They could only wish for something so easy.

"Hey, Nick…" Murdock called without energy.

"It's Nicky," she replied tersely. "What do I look like, a boy?"

"Whatever," Murdock said, flopping onto his board dramatically. "I'm too exhausted for full words right now. Look, why don't we just use We-Zoom again?"

Denise looked hopeful. "Yeah, Nicky," she said. "You saw how far we got last time in just a moment. We might be able to make it to the reef with this next burst."

"Aye, I'm in!" Scotty called from above. "I'm about two seconds from catching a ride on Murdock's board."

"Shah right," Murdock said, waving his arms in a blocking motion. "Any other time, bro, I'd say, 'Yeah, sure, hop on.' But I'm about to pass out. Not gonna lie to you guys: Bein' back in Cali's sounding pretty good right about now."

Ignoring Murdock, Scotty suddenly dropped and perched himself on Murdock's board. "Ahh," Scotty said, sighing. "Now that's dandy!"

Suddenly, Murdock hopped back to his feet, flinging his arms out to his sides. "Whoa!" he cried, as his board suddenly picked up speed on the wave. Despite his exhaustion, he laughed. "Nothing like some speed to get back some energy."

Squawking indignantly, Scotty spread his wings and coasted back up. "Ya could give a bird some warning," he said gruffly.

Murdock laughed as the wave slowed, and came back down to a sitting position. "Just goes to show," he said. "You can't predict the radical moods of the seas."

"Fat lot of good that does me," Scotty snapped.

"Okay, we're all tired," said Nicky. She yawned widely, pulling out a Chinese fan from her shell and covering her mouth. "Sorry," she said, slipping the fan back inside. "That wasn't on purpose. The point is that I'm not sure how many times I'll be able to carry us all. If we use We-Zoom again, we risk it being our last time. What if we need it in the future?"

"Why would we need it again if it gets us to Davies Reef?" argued Denise. "I mean, we get there, get the Diamond, end of story."

Kilo didn't have the heart to tell her it might be much more complicated than that. All he said was, "We just never know. That's the problem."

"Problem shmoblem," Murdock said, splashing water on his face as if to wake himself up. "We'll figure that out then. That's what I say."

"No," Nicky said. "We can't use it again yet. Neptune said—"

"Did Neptune put *you* in charge?" Scotty snapped. "I don't think so, lassy! Besides, you all got me going with your stupid motto. Don't change your minds now." He paused, narrowing his eyes. "The good King said we're a team and that we have to make decisions together."

Kilo Killer Whale didn't remember Neptune ever saying the last part in as many words, but he knew Scotty was right. No single one of them was the leader. Still, he sided with Nicky. "Why don't we vote on it?" he asked.

"Fine!" Denise said. "Whoever votes to use We-Zoom, raise their fin." She looked at Scotty. "Or wings." She glanced at Murdock. "Or paws—whatever! You guys know what I mean." Denise Dolphin raised her fin as high as it would go.

Polly Puffer Fish bashfully raised her fin.

Murdock Sea Otter stood on his board and raised both hairy front paws.

Scotty Sea Gull said, "Yeah, guys--I'm flying. I can't exactly raise one wing without plummeting, but count me in."

Nicky looked around, her gaze finally landing on Kilo. "How about you?" she asked.

"I think we should wait," Kilo said, ignoring the glares of his teammates.

"Well, then, it's settled," Nicky said. "We're waiting."

"Hey!" Denise and Murdock objected simultaneously.

"That's not very democratic," Scotty muttered.

"It's a mass thing," Nicky explained obscurely, looking at Kilo. Her furtive eyes made it clear that it was just an excuse.

"Whatever," Denise said, swimming forward angrily.

The team lapsed into silence again as rain started falling. *Oh, great,* Scotty thought, straining to see. *Flying at night—and now the weather's working against me!* Before long, the rain escalated into a full-blown thunderstorm, transforming the sea into something roiling and alive. In the distance, lightning streaked jaggedly across the sky. Scotty couldn't help feeling sorry for Murdock, the only one of the team whom the frothy, unpredictable waves affected. But Murdock was doing a fine job, Scotty noted with admiration. It almost looked like he was riding a single, unstoppable wave.

Scotty squinted in the next flash of lighting. He thought he'd seen... The sky lit up again, and this time he was sure: a mother pelican trying to catch up with her babies in the rough water, a plastic soda-pack holder wrapped around her bill. Scotty felt a rush of anger—what bird hadn't been caught in one of those at some point?—and instinctively dove toward her. Not an easy task in rain that made seeing anything difficult.

"Hang on a sec!" Scotty yelled, though he wasn't sure she heard him over the roaring water. He struggled to get closer, but he'd lost sight of her. Hovering only feet above the water, he sputtered when a wave knocked him in the face. Then the brilliant streaks of lightning illuminated his way again, and Scotty saw that she was just a little ahead of him. Her babies, however, were nowhere to be seen.

Finally, Scotty got close enough to take one corner of the ragged soda pack holder in his beak. Exhausted though he was, something was propelling him to help. What he hadn't counted on was the silly pelican trying to fight him off.

"Hey!" she yelled muffled through her closed beak, flapping her wings in a panic. "What are you doing? Get off of me!"

"Hold! On!" he managed from around the plastic. Another wave splashed him in the face, and he struggled to breathe.

"Help!" the pelican cried, looking frantically around the ocean for a potential savior. "Help! He's—"

"Trying to *save* you!" Scotty shouted, struggling to lift the plastic from her writhing head.

Once it was off, she looked at him sheepishly in the falling rain. "Oh," she sighed, giving a little shake of her head and shoulders. "That's so much better. Thank you. Now—my little ones!"

Scotty tried to say you're welcome, but all he could manage was a nod of his head. Without another word, the mother pelican took off at full speed to find her babies, leaving Scotty to flit around with the plastic dangling from his beak.

"Great," he muttered through the plastic. "Now what do I do with this?"

Soaring higher and blinking hard against the water, Scotty could just make out the outline of a small ship nearby. At least, he thought it was a ship; he really couldn't be too sure in this horrible weather. Either way, he needed to find somewhere to leave the soda pack holder and get back to the team, who were probably freaking out about his absence right about now.

In reality, it was raining so hard that no one even noticed Scotty was gone. Murdock was straining to keep his footing, and the others were swimming deeper to avoid the crashing surf. Of course, they had their own problems down there, where the heavy rainfall and swirling waters had formed tricky currents.

Polly Puffer Fish was having the most trouble staying on track; even Nicky Nautilus was swimming in a straighter line, and she was much smaller than Polly. Polly didn't understand that. Maybe Nicky had a little motor in her shell that was propelling her along so smoothly. Maybe—

"Oof!" Polly gasped as another fish suddenly crashed into her.

"Oh!" the fish said distractedly, chancing a glance behind her. "Sorry! Didn't meant to hit you...but I think I'm being followed." The fish turned back to Polly, and her eyes flashed with recognition. "Oh, *hi!*" she exclaimed.

Polly looked at the fish blankly.

"Remember me?" the fish asked. "You saved me from the fishing wire!"

Denise, Nicky, and Kilo looked on curiously, and Polly felt a rush of shock. "No, no," Polly stammered. "That not you!"

"What do you mean?" the fish said. "Of course it's me. I'm Angie Angelfish, remember?"

Polly couldn't stop staring at Angie. The voice was the same, but rather than the vibrant blue and yellow they had been earlier, Angie's scales were now a dull gray and beige. But—how was that possible?

Casting another quick glance in the direction she'd just come from, Angie squealed, "Ooh, gotta go! Maybe we'll bump into each other again some time." Before Polly had a chance to say anything in return, Angie sped off in a soft grayish blur.

"Polly?" Denise asked, coming closer. "How do you know her? What's wrong? You look funny."

Still looking after Angie, Polly said, "Colors—she angelfish, but not colorful. Anymore." She turned to Denise, hoping her friend understood. Then her heart dropped. Now that she looked—*really* looked—Denise Dolphin's colors, too, seemed faded. Polly desperately stared at the others and everything around them. The coral, the school of clownfish gliding by—everything just looked worn, bleached out!

"Huh?" Denise said still trying to understand Polly's comment. She looked at the others. "Did anyone else get that?"

"Look!" Polly exclaimed, gesturing with her little fin. "Look at everything. Look at you! No more colors!"

Denise glanced at herself dubiously and then did a shocked double take. "What? Oh, no. Oh, no!" Her voice rose in fear as she realized that she was no longer the brilliant blue she'd always been. She was...gray. Boring, muted, gloomy gray!

"Okay," Nicky Nautilus said in a low voice, looking around. "What's going on?"

They all looked at each other in stunned silence, and no one paid any attention when Scotty Sea Gull returned, calling to them insistently from the air.

"But—but—" Denise wailed. "Nothing matches with *faded!*"

"There are bigger problems than that, Denise!" Kilo Killer Whale snapped, and everyone looked at him, astounded. "Could this—could this have anything to do with the Diamond's theft?" he wondered out loud.

No one had an answer, and Kilo couldn't help thinking of the beautiful colors of the Northern lights as they blended and reflected with the ocean in his home. Would he ever see them again? Before he even realized it, Kilo was thrashing around and yelling angrily. "No!" he bellowed. "This *cannot* be happening! The ocean is dying!"

Everyone moved away from Kilo's wild motions, and Scotty called from above, louder, "Guys! Listen! We have company—sharks!"

Raiden Shark was so close to the Diamond that he could almost feel the blissful darkness of the ocean that could exist once he destroyed the stone. How that little fish had managed to escape his gang for this long was beyond him, but since she had shot past them back in the Philippines Sea, they had been hot on her tail.

"Where did she go?" Raiden Shark yelled at his brother Sam, who was just ahead of him. "She was right in front of us a minute ago!"

"Could she be hiding?" Stan, his best friend asked, looking around. "Those little fish do that, you know. They hide."

Raiden glared at him. "You don't say!"

"Okay, okay," Sam said, doubling back and patting Raiden on the shoulder. "Calm down. We've got another problem."

"Now what?" Raiden asked. He was tired, hungry, and he wanted that Diamond! If one more thing stood in their way…

"Neptune's team," Sam said, gesturing ahead of them. "They're all huddled around, and the whale's doing some weird ocean acrobatics."

"Not very graceful," Stan added, squinting and tilting his head.

"How did they get ahead of us?" Raiden asked. Then, his eyes flashing: "Do you think they found her? I mean—could that be, like, his dance of celebration?" His voice rose in dismay as he swam harder toward the group.

"No way," Sam said, keeping pace. "Nothing that clumsy could be celebratory."

"Celebratory?" Raiden asked. "Like, smart?"

"No, not cerebral," Sam said patiently. "You know—in celebration. It doesn't matter. They haven't found the Diamond," he said confidently.

"There she is!" Stan shouted suddenly. "Look, the little fish! By that boat!"

Raiden's heart soared in new hope, and then, right in front of their eyes, a huge wave swept the Diamond's little thief into a rocking, tumbling human boat!

Polly Puffer Fish was hyperventilating, crushing herself into Kilo's side. To her horror, it wasn't just *any* shark gliding toward them at breakneck speed; it was the one shark she feared most in the world, the one shark that seemed to take the most pleasure in chasing her—the one with the horns!

"It's him!" she gasped, squeezing her eyes shut as Raiden Shark and his lackeys drew ominously closer.

Kilo pressed Polly close, but to the group's surprise, the three sharks just sped right past them without a word, their eyes locked in concentration.

"Uh," Murdock Sea Otter said. "That was anticlimactic."

"No," Scotty yelled from above, watching the sharks. They were definitely heading toward something specific, something nearby... "I think there's something else going on. And I'm going to go find out what it is!"

"Wait, Scotty!" Nicky Nautilus attempted, but he paid no attention and immediately headed off to follow the sharks.

"How do you know that shark, Polly?" Kilo Killer Whale asked.

Slowly starting to breathe more regularly, Polly explained simply, "He chase me—lots."

Denise looked at Polly sympathetically. "Well, that must be awful," she said, her voice unexpectedly gentle.

"Is," Polly nodded. "Is awful."

"Not nearly as awful as those ridiculous outfits they're wearing, though! Hey—you never told us how you knew Angie," Denise said, cocking her head.

Polly brightened, realizing she'd never told the team about her bubbles! "Well—" she began.

But at that moment, Scotty Sea Gull returned, breathless. "You guys aren't going to believe this! Polly, your friend without the colors—she got swept up onto that boat, and she's floppin' around on deck! For some reason, that's where the sharks are headin', too."

"What is going *on*?" Kilo Killer Whale said. It seemed like everything was suddenly happening at once, too quickly for any of them to make sense of the pieces.

"I don't know," Nicky Nautilus replied slowly. "But I think we should find out. Come on, team!" Her brown eyes bright with new adrenaline, she took off toward the boat—and the sharks—with the rest of the group at her side.

As they approached the ship, Denise Dolphin could hear human screams mingling with another kind of scream—something softer, fainter. Something that sounded more like—

"Angie!" Polly yelled. "She need help," Polly said desperately to the team.

"Right," Nicky said after a second's hesitation. "Kilo, try to shield the ship from the waves with your body so Scotty can swoop down and grab her!"

With fierce determination, Kilo Killer Whale began to position himself before the ship—and then, before Kilo even had a chance to blink, Raiden Shark rammed straight into him, horns first. "You've gotta be kidding me!" Kilo said, startled but unhurt.

Denise Dolphin looked incredulous, staring after Raiden. "Can't he see that you're not just any whale...you're a *killer whale*?"

Kilo turned back just in time to see the shark slamming against the boat at full strength, puncturing the side with his horns and ravaging the steel. The intention was clear: Raiden wanted to sink the boat.

Chapter Seven

Kilo!" Nicky Nautilus shouted. "Get back into place!"

Kilo Killer Whale nodded, tearing his gaze away from the angry shark. As the men's voices rose onboard, urgently yelling commands at each other, Kilo once again positioned his body in front of the boat, rising far enough above the surface to block the huge, hungry waves that were bashing it so hard.

"How's that?" Kilo yelled, as a wave crashed into his side.

"That's great, Kilo!" Nicky yelled back, looking from the boat to her massive friend. "Just keep blocking!"

Meanwhile, Denise Dolphin swam up close to Raiden Shark and butted him hard with her nose, completely disregarding his suit of armor. "What are you *doing*?" she yelled furiously. "You're going to sink this boat!"

Raiden bared his rows of pointy teeth at her, but he backed away to join the other two, smaller sharks. "The Diamond's thief is on deck, and if we have to destroy the boat—and a few humans—to get to her, that's fine by me!"

Denise glared at Raiden and his bumbling compatriots. "How do you know about the Diamond?" Denise demanded. With narrowed eyes, she approached the three sharks again, hoping to keep them talking long enough to back them away from the boat. She tried not to look at Scotty Sea Gull, who was circling above and waiting for the right moment to dive down to shove Angie back into the water.

"For forming a super-secret team, Neptune was pretty careless," Raiden taunted.

"Yeah," Stan Shark joined in. He imitated Neptune rising majestically from the water. "What good are all the theatrics if he doesn't even take a look around? Take time to—"

"Smell the sharks," Sam Shark finished.

Denise Dolphin sniffed and made a face. "You said it," she muttered.

Raiden used a fin to push back his face shield. "We've been chasing the Diamond for days," he said smugly. "I mean—you didn't think all those barrels falling on you guys in the Straits of Morocco was a coincidence…did you?"

Sam Shark cleared his throat and leaned into Raiden. "Straits of Malacca," he corrected.

"Whatever!" Raiden exclaimed, his self-satisfied smirk fading for a second.

Denise Dolphin reeled in disbelief; the sharks had been sabotaging them! She looked to see if anyone else had heard, and everyone but Kilo, who was still battling the waves, was shocked silent. Then, with a dizzying feeling in her head, Denise Dolphin realized that Raiden Shark had called the Diamond's thief a "her." On a hunch, she flipped from the water in a high, graceful arc; and sure enough, as far as she could see, there were only men on the ship.

Except for…

"*Angie?!*" Denise yelled, her eyes so wide she thought they'd burst from her head.

There was no way Angie Angelfish could be the thief…could she?

As Denise was about to press the sharks further, there was a splash and then a diver appeared between herself and the sharks. It was a woman, Denise saw. *Great!* Denise thought exasperatedly. *Is this the thief? Either way, now we're going to have to save yet another human from the sharks!*

But instead of panicking and curling into a ball or trying to swim away, the woman approached the sharks slowly, her hands extended. Denise watched, baffled, as Raiden Shark's mouth opened and closed again wordlessly. His friends were yelling encouragement to scare her away, but Raiden didn't seem to hear them. He just stared at the woman, and Denise wished she could see the expression in his eyes.

Then, Polly Puffer Fish, coming up beside Denise, yelled, "Whirlpool!"

Denise took only a second to doubt herself before swimming in a fast, clockwise circle. The water swirled around her—so deep and frothing and gray—and all she could concentrate on was keeping the momentum, widening the circle just enough to steady the boat and not sink it. Seeing his opportunity, Scotty Sea Gull dove down toward Angie Angelfish and pushed her overboard as fast as he could; he was terrified it was already too late.

Angie hit the water and sunk into Denise's whirlpool, shooting past another diver who was trying to plug the holes in the boat. "Angie!" Polly cried, trying to catch up to her friend while staying on the fringes of the whirlpool. She couldn't tell if Angie was swimming on her own or just being pulled down by Denise's current.

"Denise, Kilo, we're good!" Nicky Nautilus's voice came dimly to them both, as Denise breathlessly and dizzily came to a halt, and Kilo Killer Whale slowly allowed himself to submerge once again.

"Alright!" Murdock Sea Otter shouted, pumping his paw in the air. "Check it out! We did it again!"

Kilo smiled at Denise Dolphin, who smiled back with surprising shyness. Denise turned to Polly Puffer Fish, who was flitting around distractedly. "Thank you for believing in me," she whispered, but she wasn't sure if Polly heard.

Every vibration of sound and movement in the ocean slowed around

Raiden Shark. He couldn't move, couldn't blink, couldn't quit staring at the diver in front of him. He felt momentarily faint, suddenly flashing back to being trapped in the humans' tank, the bright light…and the one person whose face he'd vowed to always remember. Her long black hair swayed softly in the current.

"That's her," he said to himself softly.

"Huh?" Sam Shark asked.

"That's her! The one who set me free!" Raiden couldn't stop staring at the woman, at her warm brown eyes behind the huge goggles. His heart pounded in elation, but after a moment, the happiness gave way to anger: How could she be helping *them?* His savior was betraying him!

"Raiden, she's getting away!" Stan Shark called urgently.

"No, idiot, she's right here," Raiden replied, nodding toward the woman.

Sam nudged him. "No," he said. "The *angelfish* is getting away."

Tearing his gaze away from the woman, Raiden Shark saw that his gang was right; swiftly weaving and darting through the ocean was the little fish, already half a mile ahead. She was definitely fast, Raiden couldn't help noting in admiration. Then he glanced back at Neptune's team, still clustered around the boat. "We've got her now," Raiden grinned.

Casting one last, longing glance at the woman, Raiden glided off after Sam and Stan for what, he was certain, was the final stretch of this hunt.

As the humans in the boat exploded into cheers of relief, hugging and clapping each other's backs, Kilo Killer Whale felt slightly ashamed. He'd been so angry…he might have ignored their cries for help. If he'd been alone, he might have swum right past them, feeling justified about letting them fend for themselves; after all, wasn't that what the humans had been doing to ocean creatures for generations? But he saw now that humans and ocean creatures weren't so different after all in their love of life and their powerful, almost unbearable need to hold onto it at all costs.

As the waters settled, he realized that the group was in a strange sort of staring contest with the two human divers who had also helped the boat.

Nicky Nautilus said, "Let's get out of here," but as she turned to swim away, Polly Puffer Fish unexpectedly chimed in. "Lady distracted Raiden Shark. Maybe can do again."

Nicky stared at Polly until Polly's body began to expand nervously.

"It's okay, Polly," Kilo Killer Whale chuckled. "You don't have to be so anxious all the time, you know."

Polly blew a little bubble and shrugged her body.

"You know," Denise Dolphin said thoughtfully, "I saw the way Raiden was looking at her. Polly might be onto something. It was like he was in a trance."

"We could use the help to keep those sharks from getting in our way again," Kilo added.

Scotty Sea Gull had to chime in. "We did all see the way they tried to sink that ship to get to Angie Angelfish."

"I'm all for help," tossed in Murdock Sea Otter. "Sharks eat otters."

Nicky Nautilus closed her eyes and pursed her lips. "Agh—alright!" she exclaimed. "Just know that this goes against everything Neptune has taught me. Murdock, you talk to them. You're the one who's most familiar with their kind."

Murdock Sea Otter nodded modestly, hoping that all his surfing near the humans would pay off. Following Murdock's lead, the rest of the team slowly, cautiously swam toward the humans' small boat. Murdock waited patiently as the man climbed up first and then helped the woman up. He stared at them, trying to get a feel for their inner *chi*. The man was tall and blond with a friendly, open face and wide shoulders under his green shirt. The woman peeled off her wetsuit to reveal a sleeveless orange top and shorts—which Denise immediately admired—and squeezed water from her shoulder-length black hair. Murdock listened to them for a moment.

"Are you okay?" the man asked the woman diver.

"Yeah, but…that shark…he was the one…"

Murdock didn't have time for small talk, so he interrupted them.

"Alright, so—don't freak out, dudes," Murdock called out from his surf-board.

The humans looked overboard and their faces paled in shock before flushing in excitement. "You—you talk. You speak English!" the woman exclaimed, her eyes brightening as she looked at the man and pulled out a notebook.

"I *told* you I heard something!" the man replied.

"Hey, hey," Murdock said. "Before you get any funny ideas about taking us in for 'studies,' just listen. We're kind of on a mission and really pressed for time." Then he matter-of-factly told them about King Neptune and the Diamond's theft.

The sun was beginning to rise, lighting up the humans' smooth, adrenaline-filled faces. Murdock could tell they wanted to ask a ton of questions, but really, the whole yes-all-ocean-creatures-communicate-and-harbor-deep-resentmet-toward-humans thing would take way too long. So he did the next best thing.

"Dudes, allow me to introduce you to my friends. There's Scotty Sea Gull." Murdock pointed above them, and Scotty called down a garbled hello. "Denise Dolphin." Denise jumped from the ocean in a triple somersault. "Polly Puffer Fish." Polly puffed up out of nervousness. "Nicky Nautilus." Nicky nodded warily. "And, of course, Kilo Killer Whale." Kilo rose to the surface and blew a stream of water from his blowhole, making the humans gasp in awe. "Oh, and I'm Murdock Sea Otter," Murdock added.

"Well, I'm—I'm John," the man said, letting out a deep, disbelieving laugh. He leaned in to the woman. "We're talking to a sea otter—and he's talking back!"

"He can still hear you, honey," the woman said, grinning widely at Murdock. "I'm Suzanne," she added. She couldn't seem to stop smiling and shaking her head.

Though the humans seemed nice enough, Kilo was on edge. How could you ever really tell with them? Not to mention how much Neptune distrusted them; that was all Kilo really needed to know. Then, taking a look around, Kilo closed his eyes in dismay and stated the obvious. "Um, guys? Angie Angelfish is gone. And so are Raiden Shark and his gang. We have to go!"

"Ah...Nicky?" Denise asked pointedly.

"Yes, Denise--it's time for We-Zoom!" Nicky said back. She couldn't help adding smugly, "See? What if we had used it earlier? We might be totally out of luck now."

Scotty rolled his eyes.

Suzanne, the human woman, interrupted suddenly. "I know him, the shark with the horns. Did you call him Raiden?"

Nicky Nautilus nodded curtly. Murdock smiled; it seemed his gift of communication with the humans was rubbing off on the whole group.

"I gave him that name when he was in captivity," Suzanne said, biting her lip. "His horns—that was our fault."

Nicky's eyes flashed, and she was about to lash out—after, all, this woman had *created* their enemy!—when Suzanne added, "Maybe we can help."

The team exchanged glances.

"This is just getting' weirder and weirder," Scotty marveled.

"Can we share We-Zoom with them?" Murdock asked quietly.

Nicky pursed her lips. Finally, she made a decision. "If they can fit in my shell," she said. "Just make sure they don't get too nosy in there. And tell them to hang on!"

Chapter Eight

B ack at the pond, my bill couldn't have been hanging open any further as Christopher Clam told me about the latest twist in the team's adventure: inviting the humans—John and Suzanne—to accompany them on their mission. Everybody knew the cardinal rule: *do not trust humans.* So for the team to ignore it, to fight their inherent feelings of caution and wariness, must mean that something *big* was going on.

"Duckey," Christopher said suddenly, in a strange, wobbly voice.

"If you don't stop calling me Duckey, I'm going to start calling you Crissy Clam!" I looked up from my typewriter, where my gaze had been focused for hours. When I saw Christopher, I blinked and swiped my wing across my eyes; I had to be imagining things. But then I looked at him again, and I was sure: Christopher Clam, my friend and constant companion of the last few days, was fading in and out in his bowl, shivering in the air like a hologram.

"Christopher!" I exclaimed, reaching to pull the bowl forward. He disappeared for a second, leaving only a few drops of brackish saltwater behind, and not knowing what else to do, I shook the bowl like I was trying to restart its battery.

Then Christopher appeared again, rattling against the bowl's sides. "Would you stop that!" he said crossly.

"Sorry," I said, letting the bowl rest again on my desk. "Christopher, what's—"

"This may be the last time we see each other for awhile," Christopher said quickly, his image trembling again in the warm air. "Duckey, if it is…you're going to have to find the team. And help them recover the Diamond."

"*What?!*" I burst out. I nearly laughed, thinking I'd misunderstood. *Me,* going blindly off in search of the team. Suuure.

But Christopher wasn't laughing. His brown eyes were large and serious. "In Neptune's last burst of power, he endowed you with the gift of prolonged, speedy flight," he said hurriedly. "It's still up to you, however, to find the courage to fly over water—it's a big ocean out there. Do you think you can—"

Before he could finish his sentence, Christopher disappeared completely.

"But I'm the writer. I report what other people do. I'm no action hero!" I yelled, apparently to no one but myself. I stared at the bowl intently, fighting my urge to shake it again. This time, though, Christopher didn't come back. He was gone. And that meant—that meant I had to find a hard rock of braveness in my heart and do something I'd never done before: leave the pond, in more ways than one.

"Mom!" I cried, launching out of my chair and nearly tripping over my webbed feet on my way out the door. "Dad! Deb, Danny!"

As I raced out of the old boathouse, Mom looked up from where she was gardening, her eyes wide in alarm. "What, Duckster, what?" she asked breathlessly. Dad appeared, too, rushing out the side door of the house, and Deb and Danny splashed out of the pond to run toward us, elbowing each other playfully on the way.

I gulped, trying to regain my breath—and my nerve. "I have to go," I said. "Neptune, his team—they need me."

Arriving before me, Danny laughed and ruffled his wing in my face. "Neptune? What are you talking about, Duckling Duckey? Are you lost in one of your stories again?"

"Duckster?" Deb asked softly, standing beside me and looking me in the eye. "Are you okay?"

"I'm fine," I said, meeting Dad's eyes. "I have to help them find the Diamond," I explained firmly. "And I have to go *now*, before it's too late."

Dad nodded, understanding, though his pinched face radiated his worry. "I'm proud of you," he said. "But be careful. And come home soon."

Mom rushed over and wrapped her soft, fluffy wings around me. I let myself burrow into her for a second, drawing strength from her comforting warmth, and then pulled away. "I'll be fine," I told her. "I *believe*…at least I think I do."

"I know," she said, smiling, though her eyes sparkled with tears.

I grinned at Deb and Danny, ignoring Danny's skeptical, uncomprehending expression. Then I began running at full speed. Behind me, Dad called, "Trust Neptune. And trust yourself!" With a deep breath, I stretched my wings out to my sides as far as they would go. I'd only ever waded in it, but suddenly I pictured myself flying over the water, casting my shadow over it like a trail of moonlight. Running even faster, I closed my eyes and made one grand leap! I swallowed hard and soon felt a strange pressure on the underside of my wings.

"Woo hoo!" I yelled, flapping my wings to catch the underbelly of the wind. Under me, the pond glowed white under the sun's powerful rays, and like I'd been doing it my whole life, I let the wind carry me higher and higher still, until I could no longer see the pond or the boathouse or my family standing at its door, gaping with disbelieving smiles on their faces. I wasn't sure how, but I knew I'd find the team. I trusted Neptune, even if I didn't trust myself yet.

With a magnetic pull, the ocean sucked each member of the team out of We-Zoom—and Nicky Nautilus's shell—one by one. They emerged gasping, grinning, adjusting their clothes and getting their bearings. The small speedboat with John and Suzanne came out last, and Nicky Nautilus, Kilo Killer Whale, Denise Dolphin, Scotty Sea Gull, Murdock Sea Otter, and Polly Puffer Fish looked at it warily, each secretly afraid that the humans would get stuck behind.

But there they were, beaming, grasping the boat as tightly as they could. "That was—I never—" Suzanne stuttered, looking around. Her cheeks were flushed a deep apricot, her brown eyes gleaming.

John shook his head and started laughing. "That was rather awesome," he said.

"Guys!" Nicky Nautilus interrupted. She gestured around them. "Look where we are."

Suzanne glanced overboard, taking in the miles of reef that were once stunningly, brilliantly colorful. Schools of exotic fish glided by, all bleached of their color. "It's all so…changed," she murmured.

"Do you think we're too late?" Denise Dolphin asked anxiously. She felt near tears, imagining a future devoid of color, all beige and gray and muted. Lifeless.

Polly Puffer Fish met Denise's fearful gaze and started darting around the dozens of coral formations, steering clear of the hulking mass of shipwreck nearby. "Angie!" she yelled. "Angie Angelfish, it me—Polly! Angie?"

"Split up, everyone," Nicky said, following Polly's lead. "We need to find Angie before—"

"Before the sharks do?" came a voice the team recognized all too quickly.

Just ahead of them, Raiden Shark, along with his bumbling buddies Sam and Stan, emerged from one of the S.S. Yongala's hatchways. They wore matching, smug grins.

"You're wasting your time," Raiden said, sneering. "It's over. The little angelfish did our job for us. She destroyed the Diamond."

Everyone gasped, even the usually cool Nicky Nautilus. Then Kilo Killer Whale narrowed his eyes and shook his head, thinking out loud. "If that's true, the oceans would be completely dark by now."

Denise's eyes lit up with hope, and she swam up beside Kilo. "Raiden, we can still make it—we can still save our world and Neptune's powers—if you tell us where to go!" She stared at him with pleading eyes.

"I have no desire to save Neptune's powers," Raiden growled, coming nose to nose with Denise Dolphin. "He's never done anything for me. What did he do when the humans caught me and *killed* my parents? Nothing! Probably was thankful there were two less sharks in the ocean."

Denise pulled away, taken aback by Raiden's revelation. Then, glancing at the team behind her, she drew closer once again. She tried to find his eyes behind the face shield but could see only her own worried reflection.

"You know that's not true, Raiden," said Denise. "Neptune can't save everyone when he's so busy just trying to keep the ocean livable at all." Before Raiden could say anything, Denise had an idea. "Besides… how do you know he didn't send Suzanne, the human woman, to rescue you?"

For just a second, Raiden pulled back, startled.

Then Polly Puffer Fish swam up front, unprotected. "Please," she pleaded. "Just tell where go."

Raiden hesitated under Polly's sweet gaze, and Sam nudged him.

"Yeah, right, little puffer," Stan Shark said finally, scoffing. "Like he's going to tell you she took it to the underground volcano in American Samoa."

Sam and Raiden groaned, and Stan Shark's face slowly fell as he realized his mistake.

"Thanks, Stan!" Kilo Killer Whale called, and he and Denise Dolphin took off side by side, with the rest of the team—and Raiden Shark and his gang—close behind.

"You know you'll never get there in time, right?" Raiden yelled.

"Yeah, the Diamond's probably falling into the molten lava as we speak!" Sam Shark added.

Ignoring Raiden and the other sharks, the team pushed forward even harder.

"Polly," Murdock called urgently from his board. "Where is American Samoa? Are we close?"

"Sort of," Polly said evasively, straining to keep pace with the rest of the team. "Let's just say it's the last sprint in our marathon!"

"How does she talk so normally when it comes to information?" Scotty Sea Gull called from above. He was about to ask for more details when a jagged streak of lightning seemed to tear the sky apart, immediately followed by a sharp, heart-thudding clap of thunder. "Uh, oh," he said instead, as water began pouring once again from the fickle clouds.

In minutes, the sky had darkened and the storm intensified into one of the worst that any member of the team had seen. The ocean was black, the waves rough and unpredictable, and Scotty could no longer see. "Mates!" he screamed. "Some help here!"

"Come over with us!" John yelled back from the boat, over the roar of the water. "Murdock, you, too!"

Murdock was a strange and awe-inspiring sight, balancing on his board atop the tumbling waves, his usually friendly face a tight mask of concentration. One slip, one lapse of judgment, and he'd go flying, thrown into the ocean, and who knew when he'd manage to find his precious board again? After a second of deliberation, he agreed to join the humans and rode the wave parallel to their speedboat. As the wave crested, he knelt down, grabbed the board in both paws, and leapt with it onto the humans' boat, landing in a heap on the deck.

"Are you alright?" Suzanne yelled, struggling to make her way to Murdock.

"He's fine, aren't you, mate?" Scotty said, landing beside his panting friend. "You just concentrate on not sinking us!"

Suzanne would have laughed at being bossed around by a seagull, but she was too intent on keeping the boat afloat. It took all of her and John's collective strength and knowledge to keep the boat on course—and not fly out themselves as it hurtled over the biggest waves they'd ever seen.

As they neared the shore of American Samoa, even Denise Dolphin, Nicky Nautilus, Polly Puffer Fish, and Kilo Killer Whale had to swim deeper than usual to avoid the worst of the waves and currents. The ocean was so dark they couldn't tell how far behind them Raiden Shark and his gang were, but Kilo knew it couldn't be much.

When the rumbling started, Kilo thought it was another clap of thunder, whose vibrations were echoing under the surface. Then, after exchanging confused glances with the rest of the team, he realized the ominous truth: it was the ocean floor shaking. Nicky Nautilus's brown eyes widened with knowledge and dread; this had all the ingredients of a tsunami.

"Guys?" Scotty called suddenly. "Guys! Look at that wave!"

Clustered at the stern of the boat, John, Suzanne, Murdock Sea Otter, and Scotty Sea Gull all stared in horror at the inevitable, monstrous wave forming a couple of miles behind them. Denise Dolphin propelled through the water and over the surface, and when she plunged back into the ocean, her eyes were dark with fear. "It's going to destroy that island," she said, her voice trembling. "In just a few minutes, all those people... Polly, how many people live in American Samoa?"

"Almost sixty thousand," Polly Puffer Fish said quietly, her eyes filling with tears as she swam. She imagined sixty thousand puffer fish getting netted, desperately fearing for their lives, knowing that must be how the people on that island felt right now. Then Polly glanced up at the bottom of John and Suzanne's small motorboat, and she didn't have to express out loud her fear for their new friends for the others to understand.

Kilo Killer Whale reeled in disbelief. How could this be happening? The colors dimming, the earthquake, the storm, and now a tsunami? With a cold jolt of fear, he finally realized what should have been obvious from the start: none of this was a coincidence. This was only the beginning of what would happen to the world if they didn't reclaim the Diamond—and Raiden Shark was too shortsighted to see the truth!

"Kilo!" Nicky Nautilus gasped, interrupting his thoughts. "Look!" She pointed, but Kilo couldn't see anything except miles of dimness.

"What?" he asked. "Nicky, there's no time for—"

"Just look!" she insisted.

As Kilo followed her gaze, a hazy figure became clearer as it approached alongside the swimming team, and Kilo realized it was another whale. A *huge* whale, at least twice as long as Kilo's twenty five feet. And as it came closer, Kilo could just make out the shape of a—could it be?—*harpoon* under the whale's blubber. But that meant—it could only mean—

"I always thought he was just a legend," Kilo breathed. Denise Dolphin and Polly Puffer Fish swam to his side, and Kilo felt lost for breath as the magnificent creature came still closer as they all made their way towards the island. "He was harpooned more than one hundred and thirty years ago. He's the oldest creature in the entire ocean."

Everyone stared in open-mouthed awe as the whale caught up to them and swam with the group. Then Denise said softly, "Kilo, that's amazing, but it doesn't help—"

Feeling almost as though he were in a trance, Kilo ignored Denise Dolphin and swam closer to the whale. Behind him, he could hear Polly Puffer Fish explaining to the others that it was a Sei whale, pronounced "say," and roamed around all the oceans of the world. Kilo felt small and humbled as he came to the enormous creature's side, and he couldn't think of a single thing to say.

The old Sei whale didn't look at Kilo. His serene eyes were focused on the island in the distance. "Isn't it so," he said finally, "that good can be borne of any tragedy?" He gave Kilo a sidelong glance, and Kilo couldn't help staring at the harpoon buried deep in the old legend's side.

"How?" Kilo asked, feeling a lump the size of a tree trunk rise to his throat.

"You must *make* it so," the old whale said, amused, before he began gliding away.

"Help us," Kilo said spontaneously, keeping pace. "Please. Help us."

But the old whale said nothing, only kept swimming, and Kilo realized that the more he followed, the longer it would take to get back to his friends. Torn, he finally let out a deep bellow, a cry of frustration coming from his heart, his belly, his soul. It rang out through the ocean, a desperate, haunting roar that even John and Suzanne could hear—and feel—on their speedboat.

"All the help you need will soon be on its way," the old whale called softly. Without looking back, he added one final thought. "Believe," he said. "Believe in something bigger and greater than yourself. When we believe…we succeed."

Kilo gave him a last confused glance before sprinting back to his friends. As he came closer, he realized that the team wasn't alone. Joining them from all directions were other whales: sixty-foot long fin whales, more Sei whales, blue whales, killer whales. It took him a moment to understand: they had responded to his cry. The old whale had been right.

Kilo's chest swelled with emotion, and a plan began to rise within him. He called the whales and his friends close and hurriedly filled them in as they continued towards the island. He thought some of the whales might retreat, but they all looked at him with their huge dark eyes, confident and peaceful. The rest of the team could only watch as the enormous creatures lined up next to each other and headed into the churning surf.

As the thirty-foot wave picked up momentum, Denise Dolphin chanced one last leap from the water, catching sight of dozens of humans running from the shore, holding hands and screaming and praying. Then Kilo Killer Whale yelled, "Now!" and awesomely, majestically, he and his friends turned over on their stomachs and, resting on their pectoral fins, began to powerfully move their sleek darks tails up and down, creating a reverse current against the swelling wave. Polly Puffer Fish could hardly watch, and the humans, John and Suzanne, held hands tightly, knowing that if the whales weren't successful, they, too, would be washed away in the terrible wave. Finally, the tsunami smashed against Kilo Killer Whale's body, and he screamed in pain, but he didn't stop moving his tail and neither did the other whales—not until their current combated the wave and it finally receded in an ear-splitting rush.

The team was just about to celebrate the whales' success when the strange and powerful combined current sucked Kilo and the other whales to a nearby lagoon, pulling back so quickly that the whales had no time to join it. There they lay, beached, stunned and exhausted in only feet of water.

Scotty Sea Gull called desperately, "They're stuck! The whales are stuck!" At his words, Denise Dolphin went cold and swam faster than she'd ever swum to reach Kilo and the others. The rest of the team was close behind, and they all stared at the whales in silent horror.

Kilo Killer Whale moaned, struggling to push himself back into the ocean, but for the first time in his life, his massive size felt like a true burden. Nicky Nautilus, knowing there was no time for fear or sorrow, disappeared into her shell, searching for something that would help. "Please, please," she said to herself out loud. Then, victorious, she emerged with a mass of cables and nets and a huge hose. "Hold these," she ordered Denise Dolphin, and then receded back into her shell to pull out a portable solar-powered unit, to which she connected the hose.

Denise Dolphin and Polly Puffer Fish gaped. "How?" they each asked.

"Don't ask how. Just do it and trust yourselves!" Nicky said with urgency. "Scotty!" she called sharply. "Can you call other gulls? We need to take this netting and drape it around the whales."

Scotty Sea Gull met Nicky's eyes, and he nodded, letting out a series of sharp, echoing cries. Over the fierce wind and endless rain, he doubted at first that anyone would hear, let alone come to the rescue of strangers. But as he took what netting he could in his beak and claws, a stark cry echoed back; and then another, and another. Scotty wanted to shout in triumph as dozens, and then hundreds of gulls, pelicans, albatross, and even kittiwakes soared into the scene, breaking through the rain with glorious determination. "Grab the netting!" Murdock Sea Otter yelled, guiding the birds like a crossing guard. Scotty looked at Murdock in thanks; he couldn't speak through the thick material in his beak. Then he flew over the whales, letting the netting fall over their glistening dark backs. Without any further instruction, the hundreds of birds followed Scotty, covering the whales with the netting. They worked in tandem, an assembly line of birds and netting, and Nicky Nautilus could hardly tear her gaze away.

"Great job!" Nicky called out, and then took one end of the cable, thick as steel pipes, and began wrapping it around Denise Dolphin.

"Are you crazy?" Denise objected. "I can't pull two dozen whales!" But she let Nicky continue casing her strong body with the cable.

"Give us some of that cable!" John called out. "We'll tie it to the boat!"

Nicky and Denise exchanged wary glances. Yes, the humans had been congenial—even helpful—so far, but this wasn't just some team-building exercise. The life of one of their best friends—and many more of his kind—was on the line.

"There's no time—just do it!" Suzanne, the woman, yelled urgently. Struggling to see through the rain, she stretched out her hand, and Nicky finally nodded, passing Suzanne the length of cable. Issuing tight instructions to each other, John and Suzanne began tying the cable to their boat in sturdy sailor's knots.

"Polly," Nicky said, racking her mind for an alternative plan but coming up blank. "I know your supersonic bubbles didn't work last time, but—"

"Did work!" Polly Puffer Fish interrupted hotly. "Tried to tell—saved Angie Angelfish with bubbles!" As she said it, Polly bit back a flash of guilt; maybe if she *hadn't* saved Angie, they would have the Diamond by now. And they wouldn't be in this situation. But that was no way to think. There was only *now*.

"Good," Nicky Nautilus said. "Because we need them now more than ever." She ordered Polly to go around the other side of the whales and blow her bubbles, while, with the hose, Nicky started filling the lagoon with water.

Kilo stopped struggling for a second to laugh at the unlikely rescuers. What a group they were! But seeing his friends' faces, so determined, gave him a jolt of confidence. They could do this; they could make it out of here! "Come on, guys!" he shouted. "We've overcome greater challenges than this. Get us out of here; I know you can!" Following his lead, the other whales began calling out encouragement, too, bellowing as loudly as they could.

Polly Puffer Fish closed her eyes and took a deep breath, *feeling* the whales' cries, and when she opened her eyes, a bubble almost big enough to encircle Kilo burst from her mouth, stealing her breath. Pushing herself further, she sucked in another breath, staring at Kilo, her protector, and his friends. She owed this to them; they were her heroes! Another gigantic bubble forced its way from her body, and she felt dizzy but kept pushing. Meanwhile, water gushed from Nicky's hose, and in minutes, the lagoon was filling. To Polly's joy and disbelief, her bubbles were actually pushing the whales. The momentum was small, almost nonexistent, but it was there!

Meanwhile, grunting with effort in a most unladylike way, Denise Dolphin pulled as hard she could on the cable, and the humans' boat squealed in protest. Even Murdock Sea Otter had taken to land and was pushing a whale from behind, screaming with all his might. Nothing seemed to be happening! But then, as if Denise's grunts had held some kind of dolphin S.O.S., dozens of other dolphins spilled from nearby reefs and alcoves, rallying beside Denise to help her, John, and Suzanne pull the whales. And hearing Murdock's battle cry, sea otters of all kinds took to the land behind the whales and joined him in pushing. Still blowing her supersonic bubbles, Polly's eyes widened even more when she saw thousands of little crabs breaking out of the sand, taking stock of the situation and positioning themselves under the whales without a word. *How brave!* Polly thought. *They could be crushed!* But calling out to each other in tiny crab voices, they formed one moving layer under the whales, pushing them along like an escalator belt.

And humans! Scotty Sea Gull saw humans making their way from the island in boats of all sizes, speeding over and calling to John and Suzanne for more cable. It was the most unbelievable, energetic, dreamlike scene Scotty had ever seen. And little by little, with the help of new additions, the team was actually managing to push-and-pull the whales back into the ocean!

"Yes!" Kilo shouted, fighting to gain some speed. "You guys are doing it! Come on, let's go, we're almost there!"

The ocean and air above it radiated with the cries of many—humans, dolphins, whales, birds, crabs, fish—and as the whales finally became wholly submerged in the ocean and the birds dipped low to lift

the netting from their backs, everyone let out a collective scream of joy. They'd done it! They'd all worked together—humans and sea creatures alike—and pulled off their biggest feat yet!

Even as the storm kept coming and the waves kept churning, the team embraced tightly, and Kilo's whale friends beamed and shot thick streams of water from their blowholes in happiness.

"We did it!" Denise Dolphin gasped.

Polly Puffer Fish flitted back and forth, crashing into Kilo's side and bouncing back, catching her breath. "Saved whales!" she squealed.

Nicky Nautilus swept all of the materials back into her shell with a proud smile, and John and Suzanne grabbed each other in a fierce hug.

"Thank you," Nicky Nautilus called out to the birds, which hovered like a multicolored cloud above the ocean. "And thank *you*, and *you*," she added to the dolphins and crabs and fish and sea otters, who were clapping their paws together with broad grins stretched across their faces. The humans from the islands stared over their boats in shock, not believing what they were seeing, and Murdock took the chance to say to them, with unusual levity, "Always remember today." Then he added with a lopsided grin: "Dudes."

Nicky hated to end the celebration, but someone had to say it: "Team," she said, wincing. "We still have work to do!"

"Well, you know what?" Denise Dolphin shot back. "Bring it!"

And with those fearless, defiant words, the team strode forward once more, only minutes from the underground volcano.

Chapter Nine

Um, Polly," Denise Dolphin asked, her heart thudding from the miles of top-speed swimming. "I think we're getting close… right?"

All around the team, the water seemed billowy with some kind of thick gray cloudiness. Any other day, Denise would have just thought it was pollution and blamed it on the humans, but today, she suspected it was something more.

She was right.

"The humans call it 'smog,'" Polly said in quick bursts, trying to keep pace with the rest of the team. "It starts at the top of the volcano and spreads out with the currents. We're probably only two miles or so away, since the water's been like this for awhile."

"So, like, this volcano," Murdock Sea Otter said, his legs shaking with exhaustion on his board. "What do we know about it?"

"It's called Vailulu'u," Polly Puffer Fish said. "There was a contest to give it a more enduring name than its original, the Rockne Volcano after its founder, and some Samoan school kids came up with it. The name refers to a sacred sprinkling of rain that supposedly always fell as a blessing before the great Samoan king, Tuimanu'a, held a gathering."

"Okay…how big is it?" Denise asked.

"Well," Polly said, hesitating, "it rises more than sixteen thousand feet from the ocean floor, ending about two thousand feet under the surface. That's just a little under the size of the tallest mountain in North America, Mount McKinley. But the main crater is where the volcanic activity is supposed to be, and that's thirteen hundred feet deep and sixty-five hundred feet wide."

"That's a pretty big space," Murdock said slowly. "How are we supposed to find Angie Angelfish?"

Everyone looked at Polly. "Me not have all answers, you know!" she exclaimed.

"Either way," Kilo Killer Whale said, "we don't have a choice. We need to get to the crater before Angie throws the Diamond in."

"Why would she even steal it, anyway?" Denise asked, shaking her head. "I just don't get it. And why would she want to *destroy* it? Doesn't she realize what it would do to the ocean—and to Neptune?"

"Me not think so," Polly said.

"Well, something like this doesn't just happen by accident," Scotty Sea Gull chimed in. "You don't just get past Neptune without a plan."

"So, Neptune," Suzanne, the woman, interrupted. Her eyes shone. "He really exists?"

"Duh," Murdock said, rolling his eyes. He twirled a finger beside his temple. "Humans," he said to the team, and they all nodded.

"Well, if he exists, why doesn't he do more to help the oceans? Why doesn't he let humans know he's there and get them to stop polluting? And experimenting and poaching, among other things?" John, the other human, asked. He furrowed his eyebrows together. "Surely that would make a difference. All the difference in the world."

No one had a real answer for the humans. The truth was, each team member had wondered the same thing at one point or another.

"Guys!" Scotty Sea Gull called, his voice rising in excitement. "I can see it! It looks like—like a mountain underwater, with clouds all around it. It's really—beautiful, actually."

"Beautiful!" Denise Dolphin exclaimed, huffing. "Clothes are beautiful. Jewelry is beautiful. A volcano that could take us all out whenever it wants to is *not* beautiful!"

"Uh, I don't think volcanoes really want anything, Denise," Scotty said. He lowered his voice to a stage whisper and flew low to the water. "They're inanimate objects. Shh...don't tell anyone."

Denise glared at him. "Very funny. You know what I mean."

"Alright everyone," Nicky Nautilus interrupted. "It's show time." She turned to Murdock, Scotty, and the humans. "We have to go down below now. Wish us luck." She smiled nervously.

"We'll be here," Suzanne said, and John, Murdock, and Scotty nodded.

"You guys can do it," Murdock added confidently.

"If you need backup, just call," Scotty said. Nicky stared at him and, after a second, started laughing. Everyone else joined in, the giggles rising to hysteria. With dawning realization, Scotty said peevishly, "What? It wouldn't be the first time you fish needed aerial assistance!"

As the laughter faded, giving way to the group's real emotions of fear and adrenaline, Nicky Nautilus, Kilo Killer Whale, Polly Puffer Fish, and Denise Dolphin said their temporary goodbyes and dove deeper into the ocean. After several hundred feet, the sunlight became dappled; after a thousand, the surface seemed like little more than an illusion. As they approached the underwater volcano, the water darkened and cooled, and when Polly gasped, it broke a silence that had seemed almost solid.

"What?" Nicky asked.

All Polly could do was point, and the team realized the answer to Murdock's earlier question: they didn't have to find Angie Angelfish. All they had to do was find the sharks. And there were at least twenty circling around the peak of the volcano, slowly and purposefully.

"Angie!" Polly cried, darting forward. All of the sharks, with Raiden in the middle, turned to grin at her hungrily, and she stopped instantly.

"Oh, you guys are right on time," Raiden said casually. He moved slightly to the right.

"Yeah, Angie here was just about to drop the Diamond. Into the volcano," Stan Shark added unnecessarily.

"I think that part's implied," Sam Shark whispered.

"Whatever!" Stan snapped.

"The point is: we brought friends with us," Raiden added. "So don't try anything dumb."

"We're not the dumb ones," Kilo Killer Whale muttered.

"What was that?" Raiden asked. He turned to Sam. "What did he say?"

Stan looked at Sam, who shook his head. "I didn't hear anything."

As the sharks bickered back and forth, the team stared behind Raiden at Angie, who hovered anxiously above the enormous crater. She was so small and gray that the smoggy water almost hid her entirely—except that she was holding something tiny and glowing in her fins, something that offered a pinprick of white light in the black water.

Polly gasped, just as Denise cried out, "That's *it?!* That teeny thing?!" Denise looked at Nicky Nautilus in disbelief, but Nicky's eyes were fixed warily on Angie.

Seemingly oblivious to the sharks and other creatures surrounding her, Angie kept darting back and forth in a panicked little line, clutching the Diamond between her two fins. Her dark eyes glinted in terror. Finally, Angie lifted her eyes to stare at the double semi-circle closing in on her, and her eyes sparkled with tears.

"It wasn't supposed to happen like this!" Angie exclaimed. She met Polly's disappointed gaze. "I'm sorry. Here! Take it!" Angie closed her eyes and, with a petrified parting squeal, dropped the Diamond.

"*No!*" Kilo, Denise, Polly, and Nicky screamed, rushing forward as Angie dashed away from the volcano. But as the Diamond fell, Raiden Shark and Stan Shark raced forward to block Kilo's path, attempting to push him backwards.

"You guys just don't get it, do you?" Kilo asked, shoving against the two sharks. "I'm a killer whale. You can't stop me!"

"How about if we invite some friends?" Raiden asked, jerking his head. A dozen other great white sharks formed a blockade in front of

Kilo Killer Whale, as Sam and three other sharks surrounded Denise Dolphin.

"You're trying to bully a killer whale *and* a dolphin?" Denise exclaimed, butting Sam furiously with her nose. "You guys must be even dumber than we thought!"

"We can't be that dumb," Sam Shark said, laughing. "You haven't quite caught the Diamond, have you?"

"Can't! Move!" Polly Puffer Fish cried, her body twice its normal size, spikes thrust out as two of Raiden's goons pushed her and Nicky Nautilus away from the volcano. Polly tried to dart over the shark, but she only managed to catch a glimpse of the Diamond, on its inevitable path into the volcanic crater…

"We can't lose!" Denise Dolphin yelled. She whirled around, trying to gain some speed to do her whirlpool, but Sam Shark cut her off. She twisted the other way, but another shark stopped her, his teeth gleaming in the Diamond's fading glow.

Nicky Nautilus felt like the volcano was exploding inside her heart. She disappeared into her shell, trying to find something with which to fight the sharks, but it was so dark all she could seem to find was a toothbrush. When she emerged, she thought, *I can't believe it's over.*

I could see the volcano from the sky, and I took a desperate glance around, hoping so hard that Neptune or Christopher Clam would suddenly appear and tell me that I didn't have to do it, didn't have to dive into the ocean and retrieve the Diamond. But instead, all I saw from my height was a boat that looked tiny and toy-like bobbing in the water. I knew instinctively that it was John and Suzanne's boat, and I also knew that the team—the one I'd been writing about for days—was down below, urgently fighting to save its home. I couldn't waste any more time being afraid.

"Goggles," I said to myself out loud. I felt for them around my neck and pulled them up around my eyes. "Check. Okay, swim fins." The wind was cool around my webbed feet. "Oh—built in, of course. The last thing, the last thing—" I felt almost feverish with adrenaline and pulled from my pocket the last gift Christopher had given me: a small can. "Salt water repellent!" I squeezed the nozzle three times, making sure to coat all my feathers. "Check!"

And then, with my heart pounding almost too hard for me to breathe, I threw myself down, down, down, until I hit the water with a hard, echoing slap. Instantly, everything was dark, and the water surrounded me with a heaviness and coldness that I'd never known before. I panicked, even as I kept sinking, and flapped my wings wildly, fighting back the urge to gasp for air. I wasn't going to be able to do it. After all this, I was going to fail them.

The silence stretched as the Diamond fell, and the members of the team thrashed with all of their power against the sharks.

"You don't know what you're doing!" Kilo Killer Whale yelled suddenly to Raiden Shark. Then, just as the Diamond was about to disappear forever, the water brightened as a flash of bright yellow shot through the sharks, goggles flashing and flippers flapping, bright orange bill open wide. A *bill?* Nicky Nautilus thought, squinting, sure she was imagining things. But before anyone could even react, the newcomer caught the falling Diamond in its mouth and whirled around in a flurry of wet feathers. As it rocketed toward the surface, it yelped, "Ow, ow, ow, hot, hot, hot!" over and over again.

Raiden Shark blinked.

Sam and Stan Shark forgot about Kilo Killer Whale and Denise Dolphin.

The rest of the sharks exchanged dumbfounded glances.

And as the Diamond shot nearer and nearer to the surface and the ocean became just a shade dimmer, Polly Puffer Fish said sweetly, "Us have friends, too."

Nicky Nautilus, Kilo Killer Whale, and Denise Dolphin exploded into raucous cheers. They didn't know who had taken the Diamond, but no matter what, it was better than letting that volcano swallow it! Or watching it get spirited away by the evil sharks.

Raiden let out a howl of frustration. Baring his teeth, he sped to-

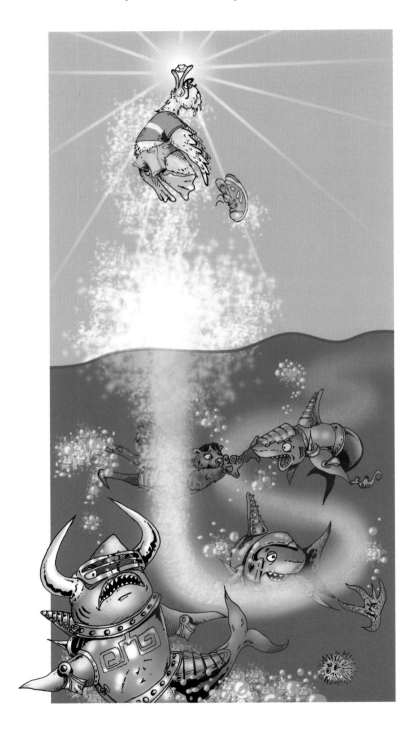

ward the team, the rest of his gang at his side. "You're going to tell us who took that Diamond," Raiden spat. One by one, the rest of the sharks surrounded Nicky, Kilo, Denise, and Polly, closing in with narrowed eyes. Polly quivered—she'd never faced so many angry sharks at one time!

"No," Kilo Killer Whale said firmly. "We're not."

"Stan," Raiden Shark said, jerking his chin toward the group. "Do it."

"Uh," Stan Shark said quizzically, looking at Sam Shark. "Do what?"

"What we talked about!" Raiden hissed. A couple of the other sharks snickered and drew closer in anticipation.

Stan Shark's eyes flashed in recognition, and as the team was still trying to interpret Raiden's strange command, Stan zoomed forward and grabbed Nicky Nautilus, clutching her with a triumphant smile. Nicky's eyes widened in anger, and she immediately tried to disappear into her shell—but Stan reached in and pulled her out by the hair.

"Ow!" she cried. "Hasn't anyone taught you goons how to treat a lady?!"

Raiden Shark swam forward until he was nose to nose with Kilo, whose dark eyes glowed with rage. "Tell me now," Raiden said softly. "Or Stan eats escargot for dinner tonight."

"Escargot is snails!" Nicky said indignantly, still twisting in Stan's grasp. "I'm a nautilus!"

As Raiden turned to make a retort, Kilo winked at Nicky and then glanced at Polly Puffer Fish. Nicky's eyebrows lowered in confusion for a second before registering what Kilo meant. Then she stopped struggling.

"Hey, Polly," Kilo said, nudging Polly forward. "What should we do about this?"

Raiden Shark laughed, lashing forward at Polly. "You're asking the puffer fish for advice? Some killer whale you are!"

Polly's spikes shot back out again, and she shuddered as Raiden tapped on his armor. Nearly in tears, she tried to turn back around to hide behind Kilo's massive body.

Kilo encouraged softly. "For Nicky."

Polly shook her head, her objections rising in her throat. Then she looked at Nicky's trusting face and remembered every time Raiden or another shark like him had chased her around the ocean just for fun. Terrified her, just for fun. It wasn't fair how they could treat her—and her friends—like such...such...*food!*

Polly's sudden burst of anger propelled a twenty-foot bubble from her mouth, shooting straight into Raiden and catching him inside of it so quickly that his smug smile didn't even have a chance to fade from his face. Startled, Stan Shark loosened his grip on Nicky Nautilus just long enough for her to dash to the team.

"What the—?" Raiden asked, spinning around in the bubble.

"Now the rest of them," Denise Dolphin said, glaring at the sharks. "Stan first. They deserve it!"

Polly didn't need to be encouraged twice. In fact, she didn't think she could stop the bubbles if she tried! Bigger and bigger, they burst from her body, crashing into each shark and encircling it inside until the team stared at twenty sharks locked inside supersonic bubbles.

"No pop," Polly warned with a small smile.

"Like I'm going to listen to *you*," Raiden said, readying his horns.

"Uh, Raiden," Sam Shark said, touching the bubble lightly with his fin. "Maybe you'd better listen to her."

Ignoring his brother, Raiden jabbed his horns against the sides of the bubble as hard as he could. The sudden shot of oxygen sent the bubble—with Raiden inside—hurtling against the other bubbles, and they all flew across the ocean, bouncing across the sides of the volcano and reef and coral formations at top speed.

"Aaaaaaaaaagh!" Raiden yelled.

"Is this a dinner flight?" Stan Shark called out.

"Shut up, Stan!" Raiden and Sam Shark shouted in unison.

The team laughed uproariously. "Whoo, Polly!" Denise Dolphin exclaimed, catching her breath. "That was impressive!"

"I knew you could do it, Pol," Kilo Killer Whale said, and Polly beamed. *Pol.* No one had ever given her a nickname before.

"That was amazing," Nicky Nautilus agreed, her brown eyes shining. "But look around, guys. We need to get to the surface and figure out who grabbed the Diamond. And we have to get back to Neptune!"

Their laughter fading, Kilo and Denise realized that Nicky was right. There was almost no light left in the ocean. Without another word, the group launched toward the surface, swimming hard, eager to see the golden sunlight cutting through the water once more.

As they crashed through the surface, the team could hear Murdock Sea Otter and Scotty Sea Gull's rowdy voices coming from John and Suzanne's boat. There they all were, grouped around...me! Suzanne was fluffing my feathers with a towel, and something bright glowed in my wings.

"Who *are* you?" Denise demanded.

"You friend?" Polly asked hopefully.

I grinned. "You can call me...Duckey," I said.

"Naturally," Denise Dolphin quipped.

I looked at Polly and smiled. "Neptune sent me—it's a long story, and I've got it all written down back at the pond, but there's no time!" I exclaimed. I stretched my wings out to Nicky, and even though the Diamond was only the size of a pebble, she had to squint against its light. "Maybe you should take care of this."

"Thanks," Nicky Nautilus replied, taking the Diamond and carefully, so carefully, placing it inside her shell.

"We're gonna have to send a rescue crew after that," Murdock said. He cracked a smile. "Again."

"Don't forget the birds in that rescue crew," Scotty said. He grinned, looking at me. "See, Nicky? What did I tell you about aerial assistance?"

"Uh, guys," John said, clearing his throat. "We have one small problem, which Suzanne and I discovered while you were down below. We're out of gas."

Nicky closed her eyes. "Well, then, we'd better hope we've still got We-Zoom."

"You know the drill, I assume?" Murdock asked me.

"Yeah," I said. "Jump into Nicky's shell, strong emotion—I've got

plenty to choose from."

"Cool."

We all peered overboard, watching the group surround Nicky. I thought of my fear and adrenaline as I surged into the ocean—and then the incredible feeling of triumph when I emerged with the Diamond. I was so lost in thought that it took me a moment focus on what was going on below. Polly was hurtling toward Nicky, and my eyes widened in anticipation—but instead of disappearing into Nicky's shell, Polly slammed into Nicky, sending them both reeling backwards.

"Uh...Houston, we have a problem," Murdock said. His voice was mellow, as usual, but his eyes were worried. He turned to me. "That wasn't supposed to happen."

When Nicky and Polly came to a stop, Nicky gestured for Polly to try it again. Casting a doubtful look upwards, Polly swam toward Nicky, this time with much more reserve. "Uh, oh," I said, and Nicky cringed and closed her eyes as Polly again rammed into her.

Murdock, Scotty, John, Suzanne, and I stared at each other helplessly.

"We're all out of We-Zoom," Murdock said slowly, as the other members of the team quickly rose to the surface.

"So, newcomer," Scotty said to me. "Any brilliant ideas?"

I knew he was kidding, but I still felt like I was disappointing him when I said, "Not one."

"I'm sorry," Nicky said miserably. "I thought we'd get one more time out of it."

"No!" Denise Dolphin cried. "No, no, no! It can't just end like this! I won't accept it. Polly, how long is it back to Neptune's palace?"

"It would take us days to swim," Polly said reluctantly.

"Okay," John said. "Let's think..." He turned to Suzanne, and she shook her head in frustration.

"Wait!" Scotty Sea Gull said suddenly, his neck lifting from being drooped in concentration. "Murdock! All along I've noticed that you've always had a wave to ride—even when it's storming or there aren't any big waves anywhere else. I gotta admit, mate, I was impressed. But—what did Neptune say? That he was..."

"Enhancing our talents!" Nicky Nautilus exclaimed. "Yes, Scotty, that's genius! Murdock—maybe Neptune *gave you a wave!*"

Despite the importance of the moment, I almost laughed at the expression of joy and awe on Murdock's face.

"There's only one way to find out," Murdock said eagerly. He grabbed his surfboard, which was bigger than I'd imagined, and hopped overboard with it. Finding his balance, he stood up on the board with knees slightly bent and arms out. We all watched his every move.

"There!" Scotty said. "Yes, it's there! Hah! I was right!"

Behind Murdock, a perfect swell was rising.

"Quick!" Nicky said. "John, Suzanne, throw Murdock a rope. He's going to share his wave."

"I am?" Murdock asked, still wearing a goofy expression of bliss.

"Yes. You are," John said happily, tossing Murdock a thick rope.

Quickly, Murdock looped the rope around his waist. "Alright—let's see how this thing rides!" he exclaimed. But when the wave came, though it lifted Murdock's board easily, everything tied to it was pulled slowly… very slowly…behind.

After a few seconds of slow motion, Murdock's grin faded. He turned back to face the rest of us. "Uh," he said, "is it just me, or would this, like, take us three years to get back to Neptune's palace?"

We all looked toward Nicky, who had been so confident before. Her face fell. "Untie," she said softly. Then, more peevishly, "Untie, Murdock!"

"Alright, already," Murdock said, unknotting the rope from his thick waist. "You only gotta say it once."

As Murdock loosened the rope, setting the motorboat free, Scotty swooped down and perched on the board. "But I just do not get it," he said, slumping forward. "I mean, I was so sure—"

"Whoa!" Murdock whooped. "Here comes the wave again! Scotty, you're my lucky charm!"

"I'm Scottish, not Irish," Scotty grumbled.

But sure enough, as soon as the sea gull had landed on Murdock's board, the wave picked up speed—dramatically.

"Wait a minute," Denise Dolphin said unexpectedly. "This happened before! Remember, with Scotty? Maybe…Nicky, get on Murdock's board."

Nicky shot Denise a skeptical look but, with a quick burst of speed, jumped on the board. The wave grew still larger…and faster.

"Polly!" Denise exclaimed, excited. "Grab hold of the end!"

Polly didn't say anything; merely nodded with wide eyes. With both fins, she grabbed the end corner of Murdock's board, and the wave rose higher, sweeping them into its curve.

"Quick, Duckey!" Denise said. "Lean forward! Grab the board!"

Without thinking, I leaned so far off John and Suzanne's boat that the cool water kept splashing in my face—and I hardly even noticed.

"Woo hoo!" I called, grabbing the side of the boat for support as we shot ahead. I peeked overboard to see that Kilo and Denise had caught the board from below.

"John, look," Suzanne breathed from behind me.

I turned around, and the sight ripped the breath from my chest. All around us was a curve of water thirty feet high—gray and curling up toward the sky like it wanted to sweep away the clouds. I couldn't believe it—we were *tucked in the bowl* of the wave, and even though we should have panicked (it looked a whole lot like a tsunami to me, but what did I know?), for the first time in days, everyone almost relaxed. The wave was propelling us forward, and all we could do was trust it.

Chapter Ten

The sun was setting behind roiling storm clouds when Nicky Nautilus popped out of the wave and cried, "We're here!" Murdock Sea Otter flopped onto his board and, as if on command, the wave slowly lowered. We all breathlessly looked around, and Murdock, glancing at the sky, wrinkled his nose. "It's the color of a nuclear explosion," he said dramatically.

Denise Dolphin glanced up. The orange-gray did look strange, even ominous, like something even worse than a storm, earthquake, or tsunami was brewing. Still, she doubted Murdock had been present at the site of a nuclear bomb. She was about to express her skepticism, she told me later, when John spoke up.

"According to our system," he consulted a hand-held device the size of a deck of cards, "we're east and south of the Marianas Islands, near Guam." He raised his eyebrows and looked at us. "You're sure that's where we're supposed to be?"

I glanced at Nicky, and she nodded. "It's where we all first met," she said with a little smile. But her face turned grim all of a sudden. "Neptune's palace is in the Marianas Trench."

"Marianas Trench!" Scotty Sea Gull squawked. "How are we supposed to get down there?"

Suzanne chewed her lower lip, staring over the side of the boat. "Well…are we supposed to literally take the Diamond down to Neptune? Knowing all, won't he just…come up and get it?"

"First," Nicky said testily, "I don't know where this 'we' came from. Second, Neptune's powers are the weakest they've ever been. He probably can't leave his palace, even if he did know we were here. Which I'm not sure he does."

Suzanne looked hurt at the first part of Nicky's comment, and Murdock waved a paw dismissively. "Don't listen to her—you guys are two of us now. I'd say you've earned it. You, too, Duckey!"

I grinned happily. Part of the team…I was part of the team!

Kilo Killer Whale looked shocked by Murdock's easy acceptance of the humans. Kilo wanted to—and did—like them, but he still wasn't sure they could be trusted the way the team had trusted them. What if Suzanne and John came out of this adventure, raced back to their lab, and came back for us all with nets and white coats?

"The fact remains," Nicky said, glaring at Murdock, "that we have a problem."

"What's the big deal?" Denise Dolphin asked.

Before anyone (especially Scotty) could chime in with any jabs to Denise's intelligence, Polly Puffer Fish swam up to her and said softly, "It's the deepest part of the ocean, D. The deepest part of the world, actually."

"Well, how deep?" Denise asked, staring down below.

"It's almost seven miles."

"What?!" Denise exclaimed, swimming in an agitated circle. "But how—" Then, right in the middle of her sentence, she stopped. A sparkle returned to her eyes, and she glanced at Polly. At first, Polly returned the look cluelessly, but then her eyes widened. It was undeniable; the two of them had an idea.

"Bubbles!" Polly said.

"Uh, yeah, great job with the sharks back there," Murdock stated, hoping they weren't in for another Denise-moment.

Polly looked at Denise. "She'll put us all in bubbles," Denise explained excitedly. "And I'll whirlpool us down there!"

Nicky gave Denise a dubious look, and Suzanne, raising her eyebrows at John, said, "I don't know…"

After a moment, John said, "I trust them. Let's do this." He took Suzanne's hands, his blue eyes alight with excitement. "We'd be the only humans in the world to ever see the Marianas Trench. Just imagine that!"

"And what if the bubbles pop?" Suzanne asked, pulling her hands away from John and shaking her head.

"Trust her," Denise said unexpectedly, nodding at Polly. "And me," she added softly.

Frankly, I was terrified, too. Sure, Neptune had given me the power to fly halfway across the world—which was the coolest thing I'd ever done—but go into the water again? Almost seven miles into the water? Without meaning to, I started flapping around nervously, and Scotty told me to get a hold of myself. For a second, I was reminded of Danny's teasing, and it made me want to do this just to prove everyone wrong. Again.

"Okay," I agreed, nodding. "Let's go!"

We all looked at Suzanne until finally, with a deep breath, she nodded.

With a face of utter concentration, Polly enclosed us all, one by one, in her bubbles, and we floated on the surface, staring at each other with silly grins on our faces. Then Denise Dolphin took a deep breath and started spinning. And spinning and spinning. Before long, she'd formed a whirlpool wide enough to hold all of our bubbles, and we started descending.

I held my breath at first, positive that the bubble would pop and I'd have to flap and churn my way to the surface, but the lower we went, I felt a weird sort of peace. Everything was silent, and we were all together but not-together at the same time, and the surface was so far away we kind of had to resign ourselves to an all-or-nothing mentality. Out loud, unsure if anyone could hear me, I started cheering Denise on. "Great job, D!" I yelled, echoing Polly's earlier nickname for her. "This is amazing, we're going to make it!"

John whooped, standing in the bubble and touching the sides gingerly, staring around him in awe. Suzanne, too, gazed at the ocean with wide eyes, and I could understand their wonder—being in a place entirely not meant for them and yet…accepting them. Denise's whirlpool was so powerful that she could finally stop spinning, and we sank lower and lower until it became as dark as any night at the pond but deeper and thicker, like it would never be light again. The only pinprick of color came from Nicky's shell, where the Diamond's white glow was growing still weaker. I started to get nervous. I was about to meet King Neptune! What would I say to him? What would he say to me? Then I felt nervous for another reason. What if we got lost and had to float around in this darkness forever?

"Uh," Murdock Sea Otter called. "Are we there yet?"

Denise cried, "I hope so! That whirlpool's more work than you think!"

Then Nicky Nautilus gasped. "Look," she said, pointing to something glimmering below us.

I squinted. I couldn't tell what it was. "Is that—?"

"Neptune's palace!" Nicky said, bouncing with excitement in her bubble. "Only it's…so much different."

We all stared, goggle-eyed. The palace was made entirely of crystal. Bigger than any castle I could imagine on land, it stretched up from the ocean floor in tall, almost completely translucent columns and spires of crystal that caught and refracted the tiny light from Nicky's shell. Taller and wider than the volcano, the palace shimmered like the pond's surface on a clear day, and I ached to reach out and touch the crystal. Would it be cold, like ice? Or smooth and warm like glass in the sun? Enclosed in my bubble, I didn't know if I'd ever find out, but the palace door, as wide as a football field, was thrown open in welcome.

"It's the most beautifullest thing me ever see," Polly Puffer Fish breathed.

"Beautiful," Denise Dolphin corrected softly. "You mean beautiful."

"That what I said!" Polly exclaimed. Then, looking twitchy in her bubble, she burst out, "No time, no time!"

"She's right," Nicky Nautilus said, her trance broken. "Let's go inside."

With some maneuvering, Denise managed to guide our bubbles inside the palace, and we all looked desperately around for Neptune. Something clutched in my chest when I thought that maybe, as hard as we'd all tried, we were too late. The same fear gleamed in everyone else's eyes as we split up to search, prodding our own bubbles forward and calling Neptune's name almost hysterically. The palace was too quiet, almost solemn. It felt empty. With a sick feeling, I just knew—it was over. King Neptune would never rule the oceans again.

Then Nicky shouted, her voice cracking with relief, "Here! Here he is!" Pushing against her bubble, Nicky hurried as quickly as possible to his side. I followed her lead, unable to believe that *this* was *him*: reclining on a sofa of coral and seaweed, Neptune looked weak, drawn into himself, his blue eyes as dim as the ocean around us. Hardly able to keep his eyes open, he whispered, "I knew—you would make it back, my friends." Then, focusing in on the team, his eyes hardened when he saw John and Suzanne, and he recoiled. Not taking his eyes from the humans, Neptune tried unsuccessfully to sit up but slid back down with a frustrated moan, his eyelids drifting shut again.

"What do we do?" Denise asked anxiously.

We all looked at each other blankly. I suppose we thought that once we got to the palace, everything would be okay. Neptune would know what to do from there. But our king was too weak to even sit up.

"I guess—let's put the Diamond on the cradle," Nicky said, unwillingly leaving Neptune's side and heading toward the odd-looking structure in the middle of the cavernous room.

Neptune grunted, and Nicky stopped in her tracks. We turned to him again. He gestured at our bubbles and said hoarsely, "You don't—need those—down here." Then he pointed with a shaking finger at John and Suzanne. "Except—for you. You two—must stay—inside."

Their jaws hanging open, our human friends could only nod. I closed my eyes and took a deep breath. I couldn't help it—a part of me thought Neptune might be delirious and that if we actually popped our bubbles, we'd all spontaneously combust. And then what? But I had to trust Neptune. So I released my breath, opened my eyes, and reached out with a trembling wing to pop my bubble.

With a sound like a tiny rubber band snapping, my bubble dissolved, and the water instantly surrounded me, cool as mercury. With a startled laugh, I floated up toward the ceiling, feeling like I was flying in space. Then my eyes widened, because when I sucked in a breath after my laugh, I didn't choke. I could breathe! I was in the water, and I could breathe! I thought I'd burst with joy, and everyone else looked equally giddy.

Except for Neptune. His eyes were closed again, and his breathing was raspy and shallow, like he was in an uncomfortable sleep. Seeing this, Nicky Nautilus quickly slipped back into her shell and retrieved the Diamond with careful hands. With Denise Dolphin right behind her, she sped the rest of the way to the cradle and set the Diamond, now small as a pea, on top of it. We all waited, holding our breaths, and…

Nothing happened.

"Uh, I expected something a little more exciting," Murdock Sea Otter cracked, but his voice was stiff, his brown eyes nervous.

Disappointed, Nicky edged away and started hurrying back to the silent Neptune.

"Wait a second!" cried Suzanne suddenly. We all turned to look at her. Her whole body pressed up against the side of her bubble, she was staring at the Diamond. "Nicky! When you swam away, the glow—it darkened. Get closer again!"

Nicky regarded Suzanne skeptically and gave Neptune a torn glance. Finally, she swam just a little closer to the cradle…and the Diamond's glow brightened!

"That's it!" said Suzanne. "Like Murdock's wave. Get closer, everyone get closer to the Diamond!"

Polly was the first to dart over, and the Diamond brightened. Polly gasped. "You see?" she asked uncertainly.

"Yes!" John said. "Yes, look! Suzanne's right—everyone get over there!"

Murdock, Scotty, and I sped closer, and John and Suzanne nudged their bubbles toward us. Then Kilo joined us, and we all watched in awe as the Diamond glowed more brightly every time someone moved closer to it. We stared hard at it, and I found myself silently urging, *C'mon, you can do better than that! Get bigger! Brighter!*

A grunt came from Neptune's couch, and we all turned to see the great king struggling once again to sit up. This time, he was successful but seemed like he could topple over at any second. "It needs power from all of you," Neptune managed. "Your energy."

We all looked around at each other. "Of course," Nicky breathed, and she gently laid both tiny hands on the Diamond. Following her lead, the rest of us placed our fins or wings on the Diamond lightly, as if we were afraid to get burned. Still cupped in their bubbles, John and Suzanne pressed their hands against the sides, and the bubbles' membranes were so thin that I could feel their warm fingers on top of my wings. Together, we all shifted the Diamond into the cradle's groove, but it was still far too large for the stone.

Using his trident to help him stand, Neptune struggled over to us, laying his big, heavy hands on top of ours. I couldn't help a loud gasp when the Diamond flashed, its glow brightening exponentially. Everyone else's eyes widened, too, when beneath our touch, the Diamond grew and grew, until its intense, luminous light struck the crystal palace and bounced out into the ocean. Quickly, as if an enormous bucket of paint had spilled over everything, color returned first to Denise Dolphin—that brilliant blue—and then to Nicky Nautilus, her creamy shell regaining its mysterious luster. Looking around in amazement, I saw the color flush back into the coral around Neptune's palace, and then the reef outside lit up, seemingly from the inside, and finally, the brilliant color seeped back into the water itself, until it was once again a deep, sapphire, sparkling blue. It was like we were suddenly swimming in the middle of the

world's brightest rainbow, and even though the light hurt my eyes a little, I couldn't bear to close them, cover them, or even squint a little. The sight was too magnificent! Neptune, too, seemed to be growing and glowing the more he was struck by the prisms of glorious color. His golden-red hair shone, his chest widened, and his eyes regained their famous electric flash. Finally, the Diamond stilled, fitting perfectly into the huge, human car-sized cradle, and we all let our breath out in a swelling cheer of joy.

"We did it!" Denise exclaimed, laughing. She slapped fins with Polly, whose wide smile seemed to light up the ocean even more.

Kilo Killer Whale released a deep bellow of happiness and enfolded everyone—Nicky, Scotty, Denise, Polly, me, John and Suzanne—in their bubbles—in a huge hug, and my bill was squished against his sleek black side. I worried for a second that I was hurting him, and then I laughed at the thought.

Neptune let out a thunderous laugh, and all of our gazes flew to him. He stretched his arms wide, and thousands of fish, including the mysterious samurai starfish and seahorses, flowed into the palace in amazement, drawn and empowered by the irresistible call of the Diamond. Even the Subterranean Guys poked their heads up from the ocean floor—outside the palace—and said to no one in particular, "So, you guys like it, huh? Yep, yep—just like we told the Chief, it was high time the old home front got a spring cleaning." Then, as if their actions were choreographed, the Subterranean Guys pulled black sunglasses from their pockets and slid them onto their faces. "Whew—" one of them said, shaking his head. "Ya think we should've toned down the whole crystal thing?" The others looked at the palace before saying in unison, "*Nah!*" With satisfied laughs, they sauntered inside to join the rest of the party. Before long, everyone felt like old friends. Even John was deep in conversation with a large shimmering manta ray, and Suzanne looked content just watching all the creatures swim by, so confident and serene.

As the raucous din started to die down, Neptune stood tall in the center of the palace and looked directly at the team he'd put together only a week ago. He looked at us one by one just like he had at the others' first meeting, only this time his face shone with pride and gratitude.

"Nicky Nautilus, Denise Dolphin, Kilo Killer Whale, Polly Puffer Fish, Scotty Sea Gull, Murdock Sea Otter…and Duckey Duck," he smiled at me, and I smiled back, just thinking of how I was going to write this all down later. "Your hearts, minds, and talents astound me. Even when I ordered you to keep going, because I was scared—"

There was a flurry of movement among the group as we exchanged dumbfounded glances.

"Yes" Neptune said. "Because *I* was scared—you stopped each time someone was in trouble and did the right thing. You even joined forces with humans, when I specifically told you to mistrust them always." Neptune's tone was stern, and we all fidgeted uncomfortably. Then he smiled, at us and at John and Suzanne, and released them from their bubbles. "It appears I was wrong. You all showed bravery and tenacity, and you made an even stronger team than I had imagined."

In the short pause that followed, all eyes turned to John and Suzanne as they discovered the water around them as I had just a short time ago. Eventually, Denise Dolphin ventured, "Um, King Neptune? Why didn't you tell us who stole the Diamond? We probably could have gotten it sooner if we'd known it was Angie Angelfish."

"There wasn't enough time to explain everything," Neptune said simply. "Besides, some things are better left for each of us to learn on our own."

"But—" Murdock Sea Otter interjected. He glanced at the boulder-sized Diamond. "How did Angie even steal it, anyway?"

Neptune's eyes caught on a movement by the door, and we all gaped at Angie Angelfish. She swam in slowly, her face pinched. For the first time, a strange, embarrassed look came over Neptune's face. "Shall I explain?" he asked Angie. She nodded slightly.

Neptune faced us all, hundreds of water creatures that adored him, and said something that shocked everyone to the core: "I planned it."

"*What?*" the team—myself included—gasped.

Nicky's eyes flashed with hurt. "You can't be serious," she said, and I felt a momentary shock at how casually she was speaking to Neptune.

"I'm afraid I am," he said. "You see, there has been so much damage done to the oceans that I needed to put together a team—one that I could count on in emergencies. So I asked Angie here, who I've known since her family was netted years ago, to help me create a worthy emergency."

"And you didn't tell me?" Nicky Nautilus said. Her mouth twitched indignantly, and for a second, it looked like she was fighting tears.

"How could I?" Neptune said. "You would be such a crucial part of the team. The problem is that I *way* underestimated how much the Diamond had to do with my powers—and the health of the entire world. Not only does it give me the power to communicate with creatures at all distances, but it also keeps the oceans bright and warm. If the Diamond had been lost for good…well, the whole world would have suffered."

Angie turned to the team and broke in, her voice quavering. "I didn't know the sharks would chase me. They were so scary and so angry, and

I just didn't know what to do with the Diamond. I couldn't reach King Neptune and I—well, you all saw me at the volcano. I panicked." She looked at Neptune tearfully. "I almost ruined the oceans, didn't I?"

"All tragedies are born from a combination of causes," Neptune said, and Kilo couldn't help thinking of the old legendary Sei whale. "And I was the biggest cause behind this near-tragedy. You, Angie, actually helped *save* the oceans by how determinedly you kept evading Raiden Shark and his gang."

Angie quieted, considering.

Then Kilo Killer Whale, summoning his courage, said, "So, you made a mistake?"

Neptune nodded. "A very serious one. The Diamond is no longer as bright or as large as it used to be."

I looked back at the Diamond, squinting. I couldn't imagine it being more magnificent than it was right then, but Nicky nodded in realization.

"So, what does that mean for the oceans?" I asked.

"It means we probably have more battles in front of us," Neptune said.

There was a long silence, and then Kilo spoke up. "Neptune, I have one more question… You told us that you would enhance a talent we each already possess. What did you mean?"

Neptune smiled. "You mean you still haven't figured out the things that make each of you so unique?"

"No!" we all chorused.

Neptune gave an enigmatic smile, and for a moment I thought he wouldn't tell us. Then he said matter-of-factly, "Kilo Killer Whale—your heart, your innate capacity to inspire and encourage. Denise Dolphin—your precociousness, how you meet challenges with such courage and defiance." Kilo and Denise glanced at each other with smiles while Neptune continued. "Scotty Sea Gull—your endurance, your decided inability to quit. Murdock Sea Otter—your acceptance; who else would have befriended the humans? Nicky Nautilus—your leadership, the uncanny way you always find solutions for problems. Polly Puffer Fish—your love and all your hidden knowledge." Neptune smiled. "Without you, the group may have been lost, in more ways than one. And Duckey Duck—the power of words, which you've always been able to access with ease. And your courage. You'll be the one to share this story with the world."

We were all silent, awed, basking in the beautiful fact that Neptune had seen things in us we couldn't see in ourselves—or even in each other.

"But," Denise said, mulling something over. "What about all the weird stuff? My whirlpool and waterspout? Polly's bubbles? Murdock's wave? Nicky's shell?"

"*Those* are the talents I enhanced. The more important things I just mentioned…" Neptune looked us each in the eye, as if to make sure we were listening. "Those didn't need to be made stronger. Not even a little."

The warm glow in my chest spread all over my body. I couldn't put my finger—er, webbed foot—on what I was feeling. And then I realized—it was pride.

Neptune looked around at his rapt audience of tens of thousands of fish, all floating side by side in a spectacle of bouncing color. Then he turned back to the team—us. "Any more questions?"

We all looked around at one another but no one said anything.

"Good. Then I can get to the most important thing. You worked together for one purpose: to protect the oceans…and me. That is why I am now naming this team the Ocean Protectors." Tilting his chin toward the sparkling crystal ceiling, Neptune spread his arms out, enveloping us all in his next words. "And you're now ready for your mission—your unprecedented, dangerous, exciting mission—to truly begin."

Neptune waited for our inevitable reactions, and he wasn't disappointed.

"What?!" Denise gasped.

"Another?" said Polly.

"Can't a bloke get a rest?" Scotty whispered to Murdock, only half-joking.

"I know." Murdock whispered back. "Like, I thought this was a one-time thing…"

Kilo spoke up. "I do have one question…or rather a suggestion. Since we already changed I-Zoom to We-Zoom, as we look ahead to future missions, I think we should change our motto, too. After all, it's no longer *I believe…so I succeed.* It's not about any one of us. It's about all of us. Sea creatures, humans…everyone. So," Kilo continued with one grand wave of his massive right fin, "I say our new motto should be: *We believe…so we succeed!"*

We all looked around at each other, and smiles spread across each and every face.

"I love it!" Denise said. "Bring it!"

"And so it is!" Neptune said, striking the ocean floor with his trident, jarring the Diamond. And I swear it glowed even a little brighter.

Now, I could say more, you know, about our new mission. But that, my friends, is a story for later!

epilogue

Pressing his face tightly into a rusting corner of his home, Raiden Shark tried to hide from the vast and brilliant network of colors and light emanating from Neptune's palace. It was worse, so much worse than anything he'd ever experienced, because it was everywhere. He couldn't escape the pain pounding behind his eyes, not even for a moment. Futilely, he adjusted his shield and clamped his eyes even more tightly shut, and Sam Shark draped an old moldy blanket over Raiden's head.

"You look like some kind of shark ghost," Stan Shark snickered. Sam shut him up with a dark look.

"Don't worry, Raiden," Sam said, patting Raiden's back and staring out the tiny porthole at the glowing rainbow colors of the ocean. "We'll show them next time."

"Oh, yeah?" Raiden asked sullenly. "How?"

"Well," Sam whispered, leaning closer. "When that puffer fish put us in the bubbles—"

"The ones without food, I might add," Stan chimed in.

Sam waited patiently until Stan's grumbles quieted. "Well, didn't you guys notice anything when we shot past Neptune's new palace?"

"Uh…you could totally see through it?" Stan guessed. "No privacy for the old king?"

"Yes," Sam laughed. "But even better. I saw who was building it: those weird little guys in capes that live under the ocean floor!"

"So?" Raiden asked, his voice muffled under the blanket.

Sam patted Raiden's back again and said slyly, "So, we're going to kidnap one of them. And hold him hostage until the others build us a secret underground pathway…straight to Neptune's palace."

Raiden's head jerked up, the blanket slipping down. Slowly, he began to smile, and he painfully squinted his eyes open. Sam and Stan were grinning back at him and circling restlessly around the room.

"Well," Raiden said. "What are we waiting for? Let's go find our lucky guy."

Duckey - Mallard Duck

The mallard (*Anas platyrhynchos*) is the most common species of duck in the northern hemisphere, and the most wide-ranging on Earth. They prefer calm, shallow bodies of water but can also be found in any fresh water area across Asia, Europe, and North America. Males have a green head and yellow bill with chestnut and gray bodies while females are marked by mottled shades of brown and tan with iridescent purple-blue wing feathers. Sometimes, mallards can be found in saltwater wetlands. These ducks reach a length of 26 inches and weigh about 3 pounds at maturity. The mallard diet consists of fish, amphibians, grains, and plants.

Raiden - Great White Shark

The great white shark (*Carcharodon carcharias*) is also known as the white pointer, white shark, or white death. These powerful predators are found in all major oceans, especially areas off the coasts of Australia, South Africa, California, and Mexico. Considered open-ocean dwellers, they have been found everywhere from the surface down to depths of 4,200 feet. These sharks are marked by a white underside with gray to brown topside. They can reach lengths of more than 20 feet and can weigh up to 4,200 pounds. Great whites are known as apex predators, meaning that their only real threat comes from humans, though killer whales (orcas) have also been known to attack them. These sharks are carnivorous, eating mostly tuna, rays, smaller sharks, dolphins, porpoises, whale carcasses, and various seals and sea lions.

Murdock - California Sea Otter

California sea otters (*E. l. nereis*) are a subspecies of sea otters (*Enhydra lutris*). These marine mammals live off of the coast of central California. They have narrower skulls than other otters. Adults reach between 30-100 pounds, making them the largest members of the weasel family. California sea otters have a very thick coat of fur, the densest of any animal. They like to live near the shore where they can quickly dive to the ocean floor to find food: fish and invertebrates like sea urchins, mollusks, and crustaceans. One of the few mammals to use tools, otters use rocks to dislodge their prey and open shells. Unfortunately, because they were hunted for their fur between 1741 and 1911, sea otters are still considered an endangered species.

Kilo - Killer Whale

Killer whales or orcas (*Orcinus orca*) are the largest species of the oceanic dolphin family. They are also called blackfish or seawolf, because they hunt in packs. Killer whales live in all the world's oceans, from the frigid Arctic and Antarctic regions to warm, tropical seas. Orcas have a black back, white chest and sides, and a white patch above and behind the eye. Calves are born with a yellowish or orange tint, which fades to white. Males typically reach 19-26 feet in length and weigh more than 6 tons. Females are smaller, about 16-23 feet, and a weigh about 4 to 5 tons. However, adult orcas have been known to reach 16,000 pounds. Traveling at up to 35 mph, they are skilled predators who eat everything from fish to marine mammals like sea lions, seals, and even large whales and some sharks.

Denise - Blue Dolphin

Blue or striped dolphins (*Stenella coeruleoalba*) are an abundant species that like temperate or tropical, off-shore waters. These particular dolphins are found in the North and South Atlantic Oceans, including the Mediterranean and Gulf of Mexico, the Indian Ocean, and the Pacific Ocean. Their colorations make them easy to spot. With a dark back, bluish-gray sides, off-white or pinkish undersides, three stripes behind each eye and bluish-gray stripes running from their sides to the dorsal fins, the blues are the most colorful dolphins. They weigh about 22 pounds at birth. Females grow to 6-8 feet, weighing up to 330 pounds. Males grow to 8-8 ½ feet, weighing over 350 pounds. Their diet includes mostly shrimp and squid.

polly - puffer fish

Puffer fish (*Tetraodontidae*) comprise a large family (121 species) of salt and fresh water fish, including puffers, balloonfish, blowfish, and others. They are the second most poisonous vertebrate in the world, with their skin and certain internal organs being highly toxic to humans. While these fish are found in waters all over the world (except for cold, arctic areas), puffer fish are most common to the tropics. These fish remain relatively small and are frequent "pets" in many fish tanks, due to their playful, curious nature. When they "puff," they expand to 2 to 3 times their normal size. In captivity and in the wild, they eat primarily red worms, crustaceans and mollusks, using their few but powerful teeth to crack the shells.

nicky - nautilus

Nautilus (from Greek *ναυτίλος*, 'sailor') is the common name of any marine creatures of the cephalopod family *Nautilidae*. Having survived relatively unchanged for millions of years in oceans all around the world, nautiluses are often considered to be "living fossils." Nautilus shells allow them to adapt well to various environments. They reach between 6-10 inches in diameter and are marked by irregular brown and tan stripes. The nautilus can withdraw completely into its shell and cover the opening with its tentacles—up to ninety of them. The shell itself is a strong and pressure-resistant external skeleton. Sucking water in and out of the shell provides a sort of jet propulsion, allowing them to move in depths between 300-900 feet below the ocean's surface. In the shallower waters they feed on shrimp, fish and small crustaceans.

Scotty - Seagull

Seagulls (family *Laridae*) live in large, densely packed colonies in coastal regions all around the world. They are medium to large birds, usually gray and/or white with black markings on their heads or wings. With a variety of species, they range in size from just over 4 ounces and 11 inches to nearly 4 pounds and 30 inches. The seagull's webbed feet and longish, strong bill makes it a resourceful, carnivorous scavenger on land and sea. In search of live food or mere scraps, they eat anything from fish and crabs to garbage, often swarming around beach-goers in search of food.

Christopher - Clam

Many types of clams inhabit fresh and saltwater areas worldwide, always living beneath the sand. They are simply classified as one of the numerous kinds of bivalve mollusks (in the company of oysters, mussels, and scallops). Clam shells consist of two halves connected by a hinge joint and a ligament and muscles. Clams have no head and usually no eyes, but they do have other major organs, which are surrounded by watery blood that contains necessary nutrients and oxygen. They survive by filter feeding, straining plankton out of the water. They, themselves, frequently become food to small sharks, squid…and humans.

About the Authors

John Sexton

John grew up in North Carolina. He came from a long-line of hard-working people who understood the importance of their role as it related to others in their environment, and as a result, learned at an early age the value of respecting the world around him, as well as its inhabitants. As a kid, he spent countless hours in the company he found most inspiring… the wild creatures of the land, sea, and air. In those early years, the animals he loved became lifelike characters to him and started playing out their lives in his imagination.

During an eight-year stint in the Army and Air Force, John kept his characters alive. While stationed in Okinawa, he met a Korean youngster and budding artist who created images for his characters. Later, as a business owner, he spent much of his free time developing story ideas and notes on his characters. A keen observer of human nature, John has found inspiration for each and every one of his characters from actual people or animals in his life.

Knowing he had a vision to share with the world, John partnered with Writers of the Round Table to finally put in motion the story of "Duckey and the Ocean Protectors," a meeting of the minds he describes as, "…a dream come true…people who are as excited about my characters and their story as I am." It is John's hope that his long awaited story will both empower children to realize their role in the future of our planet and encourage them to nurture their own goals.

KATIE GUTIERREZ

The owner of Legacy Editorial Consulting, Katie Gutierrez is rarely as happy as when she's writing. Katie has contributed to numerous magazines and anthologies, including People, Narrative, and #1 The New York Times bestseller "Chicken Soup for the Soul." She has also edited nearly 20 fiction and nonfiction books by emerging and established writers. Katie began working with Writers of the Round Table in 2007, and "Duckey and the Ocean Protectors" is her first fiction manuscript with the company. Also an M.F.A. candidate at Texas State University, Katie lives in Austin, Texas, with her husband, Colin J. Painter, and their very strange English bulldog, Mackey.

MACIEJ ZAJAC

Maciej Zajac was born and raised in Poland where he completed his art education. During his professional career abroad he worked for one of the largest advertising companies and collaborated with many leading Polish artists like: Michal Wladyka, Pawel Tryzno, Tadeusz Piechura and Jan Zelinski. At that time he developed a series of comic books and illustrated an educational book written by the Polish Prime Minister Marek Belka.

Maciej came to the United States in 2000 to be closer to his family and currently he is living and working in Washington, DC. He specializes in comic and children's book illustration. His portfolio also includes: history, portraits, caricatures, humor, cartoons and fantasy drawings.

His most recent work includes: "Hoonraki Moon," "Children's Short

Stories" by Sheila Helliwell, "Bugaroos" by Garry De Armond, "Mysterious Box" by Andrea Chapman, "The Adventure of Robert Charles" by Charles Moulden, "Rain Drops" by Ping Zang, "Otis and Oscar" by Alicia Kirschenheiter, "I am Allergic" by Dara Holness, "Wordlotto," "The Fat Cowboy" by Tom Lopilato, "Why Do We Brush Our Teeth" by Timea Farkas-Lengyel, "Children's Short Stories" by Sheila Helliwell as well as character development for Robert Stanek's Book "Ruin Mist: Elf Queen's Quest."

Member of the Society of Children Book Writers and Illustrators

WRITERS OF THE ROUND TABLE

Clients come to us because they have been given a gift. When we meet they have usually just started the process of recognizing that gift and sensing its power. Most cannot articulate it. But all have it. That gift is the immense desire to make a difference in the lives of others. But how does that happen? For our clients, it happens with a book. A Book that creates an emotional impact like no other that inspires its readers to something more; something larger than themselves. Our role in this process is to convince our clients to take responsibility for their gift and to commit to being a generator for change. Once they have accepted that responsibility and made that commitment, we guide them through the process of creating something truly remarkable that will change and influence lives in a positive way and on a massive scale. Our clients are powerful leaders from all walks of life, and we support them in realizing their destiny. www.writersoftheroundtable.com

A NOTE FROM THE PUBLISHER

In *Duckey and the Ocean Protectors*, John Sexton has created an incredible tool for communities, organizations, book clubs and schools that are interested in engaging in the conversations related to saving our planet — especially our oceans. Because we are a smaller, independent publisher, we are relying on your assistance to get Duckey into the hands of those organizations, schools, and ultimately our youth who can benefit from its heartfelt message. As John was courageous in writing this book, please be courageous in talking about the issues addressed within these pages, and also in sharing the message with others. If you can help us deliver this book to more of those who need it, please contact us at pub@writersoftheroundtable.com.

On a personal note to John from the team. Congratulations! *Duckey and the Ocean Protectors* is an exceptional adventure, a story that will initiate conversations around the world, for the benefit of all of earth's inhabitants. John, you are a powerful leader, and a pioneer. We are proud of how you are realizing your destiny.

Corey Blake
Chairman of the Dream

David Cohen
Chief Executive Maestro

Sue Publicover
Chief Executive Wordsmith

Eva Silva Travers
Director of All Things Creative

Nathan Brown
Doer of Things Designed

Kim Jackson
Maker of Media Relations